THE COLORED WAITING ROOM

2018

Tia - Thanks for your support!

CONVERSATIONS BETWEEN AN MLK JR.
CONFIDANT AND A MODERN-DAY ACTIVIST

THE COLORED WAITING ROOM

Empowering the Original and the New Civil Rights Movements

Kevin Shird

with Nelson Malden

APOLLO
PUBLISHERS

THE COLORED WAITING ROOM:
Empowering the Original and the New Civil Rights Movements
Conversations Between an MLK Jr. Confidant and a Modern-Day Activist

Apollo Publishers books may be purchased for educational, commercial, or sales promotional use. Special editions may be made available upon request. For details, contact Apollo Publishers at info@apollopublishers.com.

Visit our website at www.apollopublishers.

Library of Congress Cataloging-in-Publication Data is available on file.

Cover and interior design by Rain Saukas.

Upper front cover photographs by:
Vlad Tchompalov on Unsplash (top right).
Spenser H on Unsplash (bottom right).
5chw4r7z on Flickr (top and bottom middle, and center left).
Alyssa Kibiloski on Unsplash (top left).
Andy Omvik on Unsplash (bottom left).
Photo inserts courtesy of Kevin Shird and Nelson Malden.

Bottom front cover photograph by Jim Peppler, courtesy of the Alabama Department of Archives and History.

Print ISBN: 978-1-948062-01-5
Ebook ISBN: 978-1-948062-08-4

Printed in the United States of America.

CONTENTS

Introduction   7

Part I

1: Heading South   21

2: Martin   39

3: America Lynched   49

4: Bloody Sunday   61

5: The Colored Waiting Room   73

6: March On   91

Part II

7: The Awakening   101

8: I Am a Black Man   117

9: Don't Boo, Vote   137

10: Leaders Among Us   149

11: Knowledge Is Power   157

12: Women Who Lead   167

13: In the End   175

14: Murder in Memphis   183

Afterword: Race in America   193

Timeline   199

Acknowledgments   217

INTRODUCTION

I remember the first time I saw images from the Jim Crow era: photographs of signs that read "Whites Only" or "No Negroes Allowed." I was about ten years old at the time. Those signs, it was explained to me, were a symbol of the many dehumanizing laws and social practices that prompted the beginning of the American civil rights movement. The photographs that followed, images of people who weren't allowed entrance to places, or could only go into lesser quality ones designated "For Colored People," were black, like me, and their skin color was the only reason for the segregation enforced on them. If I had been alive when they were and living where they were, I, too, would have been denied entrance.

Yet the photos meant very little to me, and I was emotionally detached from what the people in them were experiencing. I had not experienced racism at that time in my life, and I knew very little of its history. I grew up in Baltimore City and nearly everyone I knew was black, and the few white people I'd encountered in my short time on earth seemed harmless enough. I'd never been told I couldn't go into a store or drink from a fountain or swim in a pool because of the color of my skin. So when I first saw those demeaning placards, emblems of a hate-filled and dangerous culture, I didn't feel the trauma and the pain that millions of black people suffered living under those conditions. Those labels that represented segregation seemed like they couldn't have been real, even though there were people around me who were old enough to remember the period when those signs were posted and their rules were enforced.

Fast forward to much later in my life, in 2013, and modern-day racism is unfolding in front of my eyes, all our eyes. We're not reading about it in a history book: we're seeing it on the daily news, on social media, or in person. The racism isn't new, but what shines a bright light on it is the public furor and demonstrations following the acquittal of a man who shot and killed a seventeen year old in Sanford, Florida.

Social media spreads the news like wildfire and protests erupt. #BlackLivesMatter goes viral. It becomes the name of an activist organization and is chanted by protestors and written boldly on signs. It gets used at protests that follow later that year and in ones to come. Black people are putting their foot down, saying enough is enough, that blacks need to not be assumed to be guilty of crimes, to be troublemakers—or worse, deserving of being accosted by police when the police know they are innocent, or set up for crimes—that they deserve respect, like white people more frequently get. The protestors are calling for justice and equality, something that should not be controversial, but not everyone sees it this way. Some people even call the group racist, as if black equality would somehow hurt white people. #AllLivesMatter trends on social media and then #WhiteLivesMatter and #BlueLivesMatter. I begin looking out for #DolphinLivesMatter; why not continue with the absurd, why not continue missing the point?

It's been unsettling for me to think that there might be more Americans concerned about the phrase "Black Lives Matter" than about the need for black people, and like-minded activists of all races, to combat systemic racism. But I shouldn't have been surprised. America has a long history of being averse to people who decide to mount a vigorous campaign to protect civil rights and stand up against discrimination and injustice. This practice didn't end when we left behind the era of the Black Panthers and bell-bottoms. Pages in the history books of our children may repeat themes in the pages of ones I grew up with. Are we then having a second-wave civil rights movement? Could looking back at the original movement contextualize ours today?

There's a significant disconnect between the baby boomers of yesterday, who are old enough to remember a very different world, and a new generation of iPhone fanatics and Starbucks aficionados with short attention spans. Many people in this internet-enabled era have little interest in what happened two days ago, let alone fifty years ago before most of us were even born. How can we ensure that the sacrifices made many years ago to secure our civil rights are respected and understood by the generations that follow? How do we connect the dots between the struggles of the 1950s and 1960s against segregation and the struggles we face today as we continue to strive for social justice in America? I believe that knowledge of the past can help us draft a blueprint to fix what's broken in our society today, but we have to be willing to look back to look forward.

During the American civil rights movement, the media played a key role in the movement's success. The images shown on television were critical: protestors being brutalized by police, students being blasted with fire hoses and set upon by vicious attack dogs. If not for the media's role in broadcasting those repulsive images, America might not have been so inclined to become sympathetic to the cause

The media still plays an invaluable role in social progress, but much of it is distributed not on the airwaves but on the internet. We primarily consume our media online today, often through social media platforms like Facebook and Twitter. Consuming these modern media images can make us feel as though we were present at the events they show, allowing us to feel more connected to the people who experienced them. Similarly, reading about the American civil rights movement online and watching videos of the brave and courageous protesters, who were often bludgeoned and brutalized for their opposition, can make us feel like we were there with them. It's painful, but it needs to be. Otherwise you're just a bystander.

One step above viewing media of the events or reading about them is being able to speak with someone who actually experienced them, and having the ability to ask questions. There are people alive today who can remember and share what happened. There's been a push to record the words of survivors of atrocities, like the Holocaust, before this generation completely passes away so that there is proof of what they endured. I believe we need the people who weathered segregation to tell their experiences too. Their words must also be recorded as proof of an atrocity. We need to understand, and remember, what they went through.

———

The way I first learned about the life and legacy of Dr. Martin Luther King Jr., as well as the American civil rights movement, was very unorthodox. Today, it's almost taboo for an African American not to know about the life and legacy of one of the most important people in our history. In fact, many of us who aren't versed in his accomplishments have learned over the years to camouflage this deficit to avoid embarrassment. We might memorize a line or two from King's most popular speeches, so that we are ready to recite them if pressed to do so. But when I was a kid, I wasn't that sophisticated, and I wasn't great at camouflaging the truth.

I was in the fifth grade, attending public school in Baltimore City, when I first began to hear about a man named Rev. Dr. Martin Luther King Jr. Back then, I thought he was a famous singer. Yes, you read that right: For a few years, in grade school, I thought that the Nobel Peace Prize–winning leader of the movement for black freedom was just another man who entertained America. I know it sounds ridiculous today, but let me explain.

The reason I believed this was because the subject of King's life and legacy was only taught to us once a year. February was Black History Month, the time when the accomplishments of legendary African American entertainers like Cab Calloway, John Coltrane, Duke Ellington, Dizzy Gillespie, Billy Holiday, Louis Armstrong, and Nat King Cole were highlighted. Since there was no other time devoted to the subject of African American accomplishments, discussions about their lives were usually mingled together with discussions about black social and political leaders, abolitionists and revolutionaries like Harriet Tubman, W. E. B. Du Bois, Nat Turner, Frederick Douglass, and Booker T. Washington. Once a year, during Black History Month, the biographies of these colossal figures in our history were all lumped together in one big pot like alphabet soup. A young public-school student had only twenty-eight days in the month of February to learn three hundred years of African American history.

As a result, the public schools I attended in Baltimore didn't devote much time to teaching us about the impact King or the civil rights movement had on America. We weren't taught the details: how King, through nonviolent protests and activism, forced the integration of lunch counters and public transportation systems in the South, and established legally mandated voting-rights equality that changed the trajectory of America. Besides Black History Month, there were no other times during the school year when King was the subject of discussion in class, so his numerous accomplishments and legacy were not crystal clear to me. At the time, his birthday had not yet been recognized as a national holiday and was not celebrated in all fifty states. Even when King's life was the main topic in the classroom, he was never talked about with the same level of importance as other twentieth-century leaders, like President John F. Kennedy, or even international ones like Mahatma Gandhi. Although King's impact on society was just as significant, he was not talked about in the same vein as other men who were revered for their willingness to fight for the things that are noble about our humanity.

When I was in grade school, Michael Jackson and Muhammad Ali were the two most important black men, in my mind, to ever walk the streets of America. Michael Jackson had just begun to perform his world-famous moonwalk dance while wearing that ugly white sequined glove, and Ali, my all-time favorite athlete, was still a superstar, although he was beginning to age beyond his boxing prime.

The light bulb in my young mind wasn't turned on until middle school. That's when I began to gradually understand that King was nobody's singer. Nowadays, when I think back, it's incredible to me that I lacked so much knowledge on such an important subject. Was I just another public-school student who had fallen through the cracks, or was I another victim of society's attempt to whitewash the legacy of one of the most consequential black leaders the world has ever known?

Sometimes I wish I had been raised by parents who were Afrocentric, or maybe even Black Panther sympathizers who wore cool black leather jackets and protested systemic oppression. Maybe then there would have been all kinds of books lying around the house to enlighten me about the long history of black America. I wish that I had read books about King when I was younger, and about the early days of Malcolm X's life, when he served time inside a Massachusetts state prison. It might have been enlightening for me to browse through the pages of books like *Narrative of the Life of Frederick Douglass: An American Slave*, or Maya Angelou's *I Know Why the Caged Bird Sings*. There's no doubt in my mind that if I had been exposed to the literature and the history of African American heroes when I was young, my knowledge of their lives—and possibly my understanding of my own—would be much more complete today. One of the important things we get from learning history—one reason why it matters so much whose stories get told—is a sense of being able to contextualize, to see how we fit into a world that very rarely gets directly explained to us.

The stories of Harriett Tubman guiding escaped slaves through Maryland into Delaware, on their way to freedom, would have been powerful to read. Maybe I would have known more about a talented black man named Benjamin Banneker who lived in the 1700s, a clock-maker and astronomer—a rare talent for the son of a former slave, who was self-taught and had little formal education. Studying these leaders and contributors to our humanity earlier in my life and understanding their legacies could have made a big difference in how I viewed my culture and how I viewed myself. Having serious gaps in my education on black history still haunts me today, and I'm still trying to make up for that loss.

In the last few years, however, I've started to think that I may have been a little too hard on myself. I began to realize that I wasn't the only one with a deficit of knowledge about the civil rights era and the accomplishments of Martin Luther King Jr., and I'm not the only person who could've used a few extra days of Black History Month, or who should have hung around with the smart kids who read books about the movement and were more in tune with black history. There are many of us who would have failed an African American history test when we were in school. That's the reason I was so excited when I met an eighty-four-year-old man from Montgomery, Alabama, who knows more than most about that period in time.

———

Nelson Malden is an accomplished man by any measure. He is an alumnus of Alabama State University, where he majored in political science, and a member of Montgomery's famous Dexter Avenue Baptist Church. He's a veteran of the United States Navy, a black man who at one time took an oath to defend his country, a time when his country was not as inclined to defend his most basic liberties. He was the first black person in Montgomery to ever run for public office, and he distributed the *Southern Courier* newspaper, one of the few newspapers in the South to cover the African American community. He was also the barber, and close friend, of Rev. Dr. Martin Luther King Jr.

I met Nelson in 2016, when he was in my hometown of Baltimore along with his niece and his great-niece. He was participating in an onstage discussion at the Motor House, a community performance space, about the golden years of the American civil rights movement. When Nelson was a young man, in the 1950s and 1960s, he spent many years actively participating in the nonviolent civil rights movement in Montgomery, Alabama, where he lived—a local movement that would have historic ramifications for the rest of America.

In no time at all, I realized that Nelson was exactly the type of person I needed to talk with. He had vast knowledge about and experience of a time in America that most people could only read about in books or watch in a documentary. It was there in Baltimore—during my first conversation with Nelson, backstage after the event that night—that I became eager to get to him, to hear his stories. Nelson was telling me about his life growing up in America back when racism was far more blatant than it is today, especially in the South, and particularly in Montgomery, a racist hotspot under the law of the infamous Governor George Wallace. It seemed to me that Nelson could, from his first person experience, help me understand the American civil rights movement in a three-dimensional way, a way that I'd never understood it before. And this, in turn, I thought to myself, might help me understand what led to the current form of racism that exists in America. Yet I had no idea then just how close Nelson was to the center of this history. It was one of the incredible things about him that I would discover as our friendship grew.

Nelson is optimistic that race relations in America will continue to evolve toward "the Dream" that King spoke about. Even after his friend and client was shot and killed in Memphis in 1968, Nelson never stopped believing that King's dream would live on. He still remembers how thousands of enthusiastic people assembled in the nation's capital for the March on Washington. He also remembers Reverend King (as he called him) receiving the Noble Peace Prize and how proud he was of his friend's accomplishment.

Nelson spoke to me of segregation that he had personally endured. There was rampant segregation in the South, everywhere from schools to public beaches, and there was a daily fear of physical violence, even death, at the hands of white people. His eyes lit up when he spoke about such things as how incensed he was when black students in Birmingham were violently attacked during their nonviolent lunch counter sit-ins.

His expression turned somber when he recalled the footage he saw on television of men and women being savagely beaten in Selma in 1965 by Alabama State Troopers. At the time he was a young supporter of the movement, and as the brave participants in the fight for voting rights slowly began to arrive on the outskirts of Montgomery after the long march from Selma, he was there waiting with hundreds of others to greet them. Their stories of being spat on, called "nigger," and shot at by white segregationists who were bursting with hatred are still vivid in his mind. But he also talks of looking into the eyes of the marchers that day and seeing nothing but sheer will and determination. He says that they were brave and that they were willing to die for what they believed in.

These events were some of the things that Nelson and his most famous client, Rev. Dr. Martin Luther King Jr., spoke about when King was in the barber chair at the Malden Brothers Barbershop in Montgomery.

I spent nearly a year speaking regularly with Nelson Malden and visiting him often, recording everything he said on my iPhone, and then transcribing it. I was soaking up knowledge and trying to connect the dots between the civil rights movement of yesterday and the social justice movement of today. Most days I was like a fly on the wall, listening intently to the eighty-four-year-old former barber as he recounted his experiences and described his cherished friendship with an iconic civil rights leader. Some days I was smiling while listening to Nelson talk about King's humor; other days there were tears in my eyes and I was angered by the systemic mistreatment of African Americans, then and now. As I came to understand it, the civil rights struggle of today isn't identical to the struggle of yesterday, but it is just as significant.

Today, after all the pain and disappointments, as well as the triumphs, there's one thing Nelson understands without question: When it comes to race, we still have a lot of work to do in this country.

PART I

1: HEADING SOUTH

After I met Nelson Malden for the first time in Baltimore, we established the beginning of a friendship, and it was through that friendship that I began to learn things I had never understood before. Instantly, I became a student of history, soaking up everything I could about "the movement," as it was often known, and about an era that was totally unfamiliar to me. This, I knew, was my chance to finally fill a void that had been lingering for most of my life. I was like an empty vessel being filled with a valuable raw commodity, a vital substance that would soon alter the way I saw the world.

Soon I was calling Nelson on the phone every week at his home in Montgomery, Alabama, hungry for knowledge. One day, he began telling me about a close friendship he'd had with an iconic leader in the movement, and I was blown away.

"Hold up. You were friends with *whom?*"

To my shock, it turned out that Nelson had been very good friends with none other than Rev. Dr. Martin Luther King Jr., who was a regular at his barbershop in Montgomery through the 1950s and 1960s. King began going to the barbershop every week, right before Rosa Parks's arrest for refusing to give up her bus seat to a white man brought the civil rights movement in Montgomery to national headlines. As Nelson described his decade-long association friendship with King, I was in near disbelief. I was on a call with someone who was not only an active member of the civil rights movement himself, but also a friend of the legendary Dr. Martin Luther King Jr. I listened eagerly as he told me about the time they spent together in the South during a very volatile period in this nation's history.

One day, Nelson invited me down south to talk more in person. Of course I jumped at the opportunity and soon after, on a warm summer day in 2017, I arrived for the first time in my life in the Deep South, in the city of Montgomery, Alabama, commonly known to the locals as "the Gump." I had booked an early morning flight on Southwest Airlines leaving from the Baltimore-Washington International Thurgood Marshall Airport in Baltimore (which is named, I should point out, for the first African American justice of the US Supreme Court) for Alabama. After arriving at the Montgomery Regional Airport, I took the fifteen-minute taxi ride downtown to the Renaissance Montgomery Hotel and Spa on Tallapoosa Street.

Never having traveled before in the Deep South—a place that had been described to me as a historic (and sometimes modern) hotbed of racism—I wasn't sure what to expect. I had been told that the Renaissance was the nicest hotel in the city and booked it because the idea of having a comfortable room to return to each night gave me comfort. As I walked into its plush lobby, the hotel seemed to live up to its reputation. I checked in at the front desk, dropped my bags off in Room 822, and ran back outside to grab another taxi. I was already running late for my scheduled meeting with Nelson.

I didn't realize until I arrived that our meeting place was an empty lot on S. Jackson Street. When I stepped out of the taxi, I looked to my left and saw my eighty-four-year-old friend standing there under the cool shade of a tall tree. Nelson was wearing tan slacks, a white short-sleeved button-up shirt, and a vintage hat to shield his head from the powerful Alabama sun.

Just like the first time I saw him, he reminded me of my grandfather Gradie Shird, who died when I was a young teenager. My grandfather raised twelve kids with my grandmother, so although it didn't happen often, he had a lot of experience knocking young people upside the head and putting them in their places when necessary. He was a man's man and had the knuckles to back it up.

Nelson was similarly mild-mannered, with a calm and relaxed demeanor, but he was nobody's pushover. His mind was sharp, and he was articulate. I could see that he had taken care of himself over the years, and he said his health was excellent. He was easygoing and had a lot of style and class.

I was elated to see Nelson, but I was curious as to why we were meeting in an empty lot. This was my first time seeing him in person since we first met in Baltimore, months earlier.

"Hi there," he said. "Is this your first time in Alabama?"

"Yes, it sure is."

"Okay! In that case, we need to make sure that you get the chance to taste some good Alabama food while you're here. We have to get you a big old plate of fried catfish, or shrimp and grits."

One way to have a memorable time when traveling is to embrace the cuisine of your host city. The food is one of the things you'll never forget about any place you visit. My mouth began to water at his suggestion, but then, just as quickly, our conversation shifted to the real reason I was here: to hear Nelson reflect on the many years of black triumph in the South, as well as those years of trepidation. As Nelson and I began talking, he spoke about the period that he referred to as the "old days." It was a time when blacks in America had to fight for the right to be treated as equal citizens, a time when it was all too easy for blacks to be pushed aside by barriers that were both social and legal—and a time when anger at this injustice, in a supposedly free country, was reaching a boiling point. It was clear to me that the civil rights era was still fresh in Nelson's mind, the source of memories, both good and bad, that he will never forget.

As Nelson and I stood there on Jackson Street, he began to explain to me why he had wanted to meet there, which still wasn't clear to me. He told me that we were in Montgomery's Centennial Hill neighborhood, a once segregated section of the city, which in the middle of the twentieth century was both the capital of Alabama and the epicenter of the American civil rights movement. The area was rich with history, and not only for the successes achieved here in the struggle for black freedom.

In the 1950s, Jackson Street was where black people in the South wanted to be—like Madison Avenue in New York, but much more intimate. For Nelson, it was where he had a front row seat to the American civil rights movement as it unfolded in real time. Many activists and leaders in the civil rights movement emerged from somewhere within a ten-block radius around Jackson Street. In 1954, King lived with his beautiful wife, Coretta Scott King, at 309 S. Jackson Street. With Reverend King residing one block away, there was a lot of activity in this neighborhood.

At the top of Jackson Street was the campus of Alabama State College, now Alabama State University. Alabama State was like an incubator for young black activists, encouraging them to become part of something bigger than themselves. Many students who attended the college were involved in the demonstrations and civil disobedience actions that took place in Montgomery and elsewhere across Alabama and the nation. They protested in the Montgomery streets, and they took trains and buses to other cities to march in their streets. They had no idea at the time how significant their impact would be, but they ultimately became just as important to the movement as the leaders that we know today.

Before I met Nelson, the Deep South was a place that I never had much interest in visiting. Now, standing there on a clear, hot day in the thick humidity of the summer, I couldn't believe I'd never been there before. It had a rich history, a legacy etched in the pavement. In Nelson's own words: "We were young, we were brave, and we were crazy sometimes, because we often put ourselves in harm's way. But many positive outcomes were achieved during a time when all we wanted to do was to make a difference and all we wanted in return was equal rights."

———

Nelson was born on November 8, 1933 in Monroeville, Alabama—also the birthplace, seven years earlier, of Harper Lee, author of *To Kill a Mockingbird*—and grew up in Pensacola, Florida. His father, born in 1896, and his mother, born in 1900, met in Monroeville in the early 1900s. His paternal grandfather was a slave until the Emancipation Proclamation, declared by President Abraham Lincoln in 1863. One of his maternal great-grandfathers was a white man.

The man who owned Nelson's paternal grandfather was a prominent and wealthy builder who arrived in Monroeville in the mid-1800s to construct homes and other buildings. As a child, Nelson often wondered why his grandfather's house was so well-built compared to other homes in the community. Later, he discovered that his grandfather had learned how to build homes from the white man who'd once owned him.

The white great-grandfather had a wife and children, but also two other families living in Monroeville with children he conceived and supported.

Let me explain: My mother's grandfather was a white man who was married to a white woman, but he also had ten children with an African American woman and ten children with a Native American woman. The kids were all mixed race or mulatto, whatever word you want to use to describe them. Follow me? So, my mother's father was half white and half black. His wife, my grandmother—my mother's mother—was a pureblooded Indian from Monroeville.

My mother was mixed race and incredibly beautiful. Her complexion was very light, and her hair was long and black. I was very close with her. I was the youngest of seven boys, and she gave me the impression that I was the pretty boy in the family; she kept me dressed up all the time. But my father was a disciplinarian, and he wouldn't let her love for her children interfere with his discipline.

Nelson's father was a World War I veteran and had learned the importance of strong discipline while in the military. As a result, all his children managed to avoid the pitfalls of drugs and jail. Growing up in the segregated South, his father had had very few opportunities, and so he understood the importance of education; he wanted his sons to have a bright future with financial security. Starting when Nelson was old enough to go to school, when the family was in Pensacola, Nelson's father had enrolled him in a private school with a tuition of fifty cents a day.

Nelson was diligent in pursuing education from there forward. After moving to Montgomery from Florida in 1952, he enrolled in Alabama State College, founded in 1867 by a group of freed slaves. The college was just a short walk from the College Hill Barbershop, where he worked with his brothers. Nelson would take a leave of absence midway through college to serve in the military, like his father before him, spending sixteen months in the United States Navy before receiving an honorable discharge. He then returned to Montgomery to continue working with his brothers and complete his education. When Nelson received his bachelor's degree in political science, his father's dream of having an educated youngest son was fulfilled.

Nelson met his loving wife Willodean, "Dee," as she prefers to be called, in 1959, when she came in to the barbershop to get her hair cut. Four months later, on Valentine's Day, 1960, they married. Dee was also well educated, a graduate of Alabama State College with a degree in elementary education. She worked as a teacher at an elementary school in Montgomery.

Nelson and Dee never had children. Throughout the fifty-eight years they've been together, it has been just the two of them, and they've stayed madly in love. They've vacationed around the world, sunbathing in places like Aruba, Bermuda, and Miami Beach and exploring big cities like Beijing and Shanghai.

As our conversation began to wrap up, Nelson suggested that I stay the night at his house. I declined, but I was moved by this striking example of Alabama's world-renowned Southern hospitality.

In 1946, Nelson's older brother, Spurgeon Malden, moved to Montgomery from his home in Pensacola, Florida. Two years later, in 1948, his other brother, Stephen Malden, moved to Montgomery and became a barber at College Hill after finishing high school in Pensacola. So the pattern was well established by 1952, when Nelson completed high school in Pensacola and he, too, moved to Montgomery. He enrolled in Alabama State College and likewise became a barber at College Hill, where his two brothers had already established a good relationship with the owner.

At that time, the College Hill Barbershop, located at the corner of Jackson and Hutchinson Streets in Montgomery's Centennial Hill neighborhood, was the busiest black barbershop in the entire city of Montgomery. It was located about a block from Alabama State College and because of its proximity to the college campus, the barbershop was an assembly line of sorts for cutting the hair of black students, where a haircut normally cost them about $1.75. Most of Nelson's clients were students, but he also cut the hair of many professors, who were among the African American elite in Montgomery at the time. Even the president of Alabama State College was a regular customer of College Hill, and so were most of the black doctors in Montgomery. Isaac Hathaway, one of the men commissioned by the United States Mint to create the first Booker T. Washington silver dollar, visited frequently, and Nelson had five or six clients who had PhDs, and others who were in the finance industry. Another regular client of Nelson's was Vernon John, who was the pastor of Dexter Avenue Baptist Church before Reverend King arrived. According to Nelson, Vernon John was the first black minister in the United States to have a sermon published in a national publication.

Since the barbershop's clientele included some of Montgomery's black social and political influencers, Nelson was just nineteen years old when he was first able to spend a great deal of time with some of the most important local and national black figures. Of that experience, he said that "College Hill was the kind of environment that included black intellectuals and we always had conversations about subjects that mattered"—a remarkable gift to a young man whose own education was not yet finished.

In 1954, when Nelson was a freshman college student, he became the personal barber to the then twenty-five-year-old Reverend Martin Luther King Jr. King first selected College Hill as the place to get his haircut as a matter of convenience: He lived down the street from the barbershop, and the church where he pastored, where he spent a considerable amount of time, was not far away. There were other barbershops in Montgomery, but because of segregation, there were only a few where African Americans could get their hair cut—and precisely because of that lack of choice, College Hill soon became more than just a barbershop.

King walked into the barbershop one day just as Nelson was about to rush off to his ten a.m. class at Alabama State College, but Nelson didn't think anything of it. He recalls, "A prospective customer parked in front of the barbershop and came in asking who could give him a nice trim." Nelson was initially nervous to do so—he never liked to start a client's haircut after twenty minutes to the hour, because one head usually took him at least fifteen minutes. The semester had just started, and he didn't want to be late, but on that morning, he told me, "I looked at this short black man who had just jumped out of a car, and I said to myself, 'Oh, heck. I can knock him out in ten minutes.'"

As with any new customer, Nelson asked his name and where he was from. King told him he had recently moved to Montgomery and that he was the new preacher at Dexter Avenue Baptist Church, where Nelson was a member.

Once he had finished cutting King's hair, Nelson handed him a mirror and asked if he liked the cut, to which King responded, "It's pretty good."

"Now, when you tell a barber that a haircut is 'good,' that's somewhat of an insult," Nelson told me with a big smile.

When Reverend King came back two weeks later, Nelson was busy working on another customer. Even though the other barber's chair was vacant, King waited for him to finish. When Nelson's chair opened up, the reverend came over and sat down, and Nelson began cutting his hair. He remembered the unenthusiastic assessment King had offered of his work the last time he was there, so Nelson said, "That must have been a pretty good haircut you got the last time you were here, huh?"

"You're all right," King said.

One question would soon arise.

Now, most of the time, after the second or third haircut, a new customer gives the barber a tip if they're satisfied. But after I cut Martin's hair at least seven or eight times, I noticed that he never gave me a tip. So one day I decided to use a little psychology on him, and I asked, "Reverend, when you finish preaching a sermon at church on Sunday morning, and the church members tell you that you delivered a good sermon, doesn't that make you feel good?"

He said, "Yes."

So, I continued, "When you go to a restaurant and you have a nice meal and the waitress gives you great service, in return, you give her a tip, right? Don't you think that makes her feel good?"

He said, "Yes."

Then Martin said to me, "Do you read your Bible? The Bible says you're supposed to give 10 percent of your earnings in church. Do you give 10 percent of your earnings to the church?"

I responded by explaining, "Rev, I'm a student at Alabama State College right now. I can't afford to give 10 percent of my earnings to the church."

He said, "Well, I'm the pastor of Dexter Avenue Baptist Church, and I can't afford to tip you, either." Then we both began to laugh.

In 1958, twenty-five-year-old Nelson and his brothers, Stephen and Spurgeon, left College Hill to open the Malden Brothers Barbershop at 407 S. Jackson Street, on the bottom level of the Ben Moore Hotel. They were inspired by their father's legacy, himself an entrepreneur and barber. Nelson's brother knew the hotel's owner, Mrs. Moore, whose husband was deceased. Because she wanted to see young black men become entrepreneurs and businessmen, Mrs. Moore gave the brothers a financial break, allowing them to pay only one hundred dollars per month to rent the space for their barbershop. During the time she was alive, she never increased their rent.

The Ben Moore Hotel was located on the corner of High and Jackson Streets, and it stood tall in the skyline in comparison to the other two- and three-story buildings in the area. The Ben Moore had the first license that allowed lodging for blacks in Montgomery, and it was one of the only hotels in Alabama where blacks could stay. It was referred to, in those years, as "the best hotel south of the Ohio River" for blacks, and was the centerpiece of the segregated section of Montgomery.

In those years, blacks didn't have many options as to where to open a business in Montgomery. Jim Crow laws enforced racial segregation, and one of the many things prohibited to blacks was the opening of businesses outside segregated sections of the city. Segregation was overt oppression, and black Southerners were forced to live with it for almost one hundred years after the end of slavery in America. A black person couldn't just go to any restaurant to eat or any barbershop to get a haircut.

The Ben Moore was frequented by the most elite black Southerners; some of the premier civil rights activists in Montgomery even lived there. Bayard Rustin, Dr. Benjamin Mays, and Mordecai Johnson, the first black president of Howard University, all stayed there for a time while working with others on strategies to fight the civil rights battle around America. On the hotel's first floor was the Majestic Café, which was also black-owned and was an important meeting place in the black section of town and for black travelers visiting the city. Black musicians came to the Ben Moore to play jazz and perform in the rooftop garden of the hotel, which was referred to as the Afro Club. According to Nelson, the club boasted a clientele of beautiful, sophisticated, and intellectual African American women. "These were some of the most attractive black girls I had ever seen in my life," he said. "They were all from the area or attended Alabama State."

For the Malden brothers, opening a barbershop connected to the Ben Moore turned out to be a great business decision. Because of all the activity in the area, new clients were easy to come by, and having cut hair in College Hill for so many years, they had built solid client–barber relationships with many of their customers, who remained loyal when the Maldens opened their own shop. All the leading figures who were customers at College Hill, the doctors and professors, followed them to Jackson Street. When Reverend King followed, too, Nelson's previous employers were devastated. And students continued to come as well, flooding in from Alabama State. Nelson estimated that at least 75 percent of the students at the college were regulars, as well as many of the famous Tuskegee Airmen, who often travelled from the nearby base to get haircuts. Even the black military men from Maxwell Field, later named Maxwell Air Force Base, became regulars. Legendary singers from the old school, like Little Richard and B.B. King, also stopped in from time to time.

The young minds and passionate personalities at the barbershop made its atmosphere electrifying. It was one of the few institutions of business in Montgomery where black people could sit together undisturbed and talk about anything and everything.

The black barbershop and the black church were the only places we had. At that time, we didn't realize the value of the black barbershop. It was one of the few places where we could congregate and express ourselves in a community atmosphere. There were many subjects that we passionately discussed, like politics, the government, racism, and women. We could express what we really felt about issues that affected our lives. It was like a sanctuary, and that's what made it so unique. And you could say things that you couldn't say in the church. You couldn't go to the church and talk about most of the things we talked about in the barbershop. In the barbershop, you could talk about anything that you wanted, like race, sports, or sex. You could talk about how hard Jackie Robinson hit the baseball in a game the previous night. When Joe Louis knocked out Max Schmeling, I remember people ran out of the barbershop and into the street, hollering and screaming, "Joe knocked out Max Schmeling, Joe knocked out Schmeling." This was a place where we felt comfortable opening up and talking, almost like a second home.

King got the same style of haircut about once a week, often on a Saturday night, but sometimes, if he had a special speaking engagement early the next week, he'd come by the barbershop just to get a shape-up or have his mustache trimmed. While he was in the barber's chair, he and Nelson often had casual conversations about his kids, the church, or whatever was going on in the news at the time. King spent a considerable amount of time in the Malden Brothers Barbershop after they opened at 407 S. Jackson Street, which was right down the street from King's home at number 309. King would also come to the shop sometimes just to sit and read or write.

If two clients were in the barbershop that Nelson thought would benefit from knowing each other, he always made sure to make an introduction, but sometimes it didn't go smoothly.

Here in the barbershop, we often had debates and discussions about whichever current events were in the news at the time—religion, race, sports, you name it! One of the best debates that I can recall was between Reverend King and a client of mine who was a sociology professor and the head of the sociology department at the Hampton Institute [a major institution for black higher education at the time]. He had relatives living down in south Alabama whom he would visit, but he'd stop in Montgomery to get his hair cut. He was a bona fide intellectual from head to toe. One day he came into the barbershop at a time when I had just finished cutting Reverend King's hair. Reverend King was an intellectual as well, and he had a bachelor's of science in sociology from Morehouse, so I thought it would be nice to introduce him to the professor. The professor was already familiar with Martin because by then he was well on his way to becoming a world-renowned leader.

I don't remember how the topic came up, but I do remember when Reverend King said to the professor, "Morality is one of the strongest forces in the American family today."

The sociology professor from the Hampton Institute disagreed with the reverend and said, "I beg your pardon, sir, but I believe that economics is the strongest force in the American family." He went on to say, "When the European white men came to this country, one of the first things they did was to build some of the top universities in the New England area to educate themselves. When they got oranges in Florida, sugar cane in Louisiana, oil in Texas, grapes in California, and tobacco in Virginia, they built Wall Street to control the capital, and then they built West Point to defend it." He said, "That is the United States of America."

Reverend King said, "Have a good day, sir."

I think that was one of the only times when the reverend didn't win an intellectual discussion in the barbershop. He knew how to debate well, but he also knew how to have a conversation with the common man. King's unique oratory skills were never intended to place himself above the people, but he used that communication skill to submerge himself in the community, where the people who mattered most to him were the common man.

I asked Nelson if King was always working on civil rights matters and he explained that King was a workaholic and travelled often, so he spent a lot of his downtime with his family. He often conducted meetings in the basement of Dexter Avenue Baptist Church. The church building sometimes functioned as a headquarters where he brainstormed with others involved in the leadership of the movement and conducted the business of the Southern Christian Leadership Conference (SCLC).

One of the things Nelson said he appreciated about the reverend was that money was never more important to him than the people he served. One Saturday night when Nelson was cutting his hair, King had his briefcase with him, which was filled with letters from people from all over the country. Several of the letters contained money from his supporters, donations to support his civil rights work. Some people would send him checks, but others, mainly elderly people, would send him cash. While King was sitting in his barber chair, Nelson watched as he read the letters. According to Nelson, he read each one from beginning to end, as Nelson peeked over his shoulder to see what people were writing about. "He would casually drop the money and checks down into the briefcase on the floor next to the barber chair as he read, never paying much attention to where they landed. He was more interested in what the people were saying in the letters. From my understanding, he took the time to reply to as many as he could."

"Did King always sit in the same chair when he came to get a haircut?" I asked.

"Yes," Nelson affirmed. "Every time he got his hair cut here, he would only sit in my chair."

"What are some of the other memories you have of him coming here?"

"Well, there are many of them. Martin could be hilarious when he wanted to be. He had a close friend who he would meet here sometimes named Gilbert Klein, and they would always tell jokes and tease each other. I remember the time Martin told this one joke that I knew was a little out of line."

When Gilbert Klein said to Reverend King, "Tell me a joke," almost everybody in the barbershop turned to listen. They knew that even though the reverend was a serious guy on most days, he still had a funny side to him.

So he began telling a joke about a white man who hired this black man to chauffeur him around because both of his legs were amputated. One Sunday morning, they went to church together. The white man wanted to sit in the front of the church, so the black man pushed his wheelchair up to the front of the chapel. The black man sat outside while the service was being conducted, listening from outside, and he believed that the pastor preached a good sermon. So, when the church opened the doors for nonmembers to join, the black man walked up to the altar. The church pastor knew that he couldn't allow the black man to join the church, because the church was all white and he didn't want to upset any of the white members there. So, the pastor whispered in the black man's ear, saying, "You go home and talk to Jesus and come back another time."

A few weeks later, the black man escorted the white man back to the church service again. And again, close to the end of the church service, the pastor opened the doors of the church for nonmembers to join. The black man walked up to the altar, where the pastor was standing, and the pastor asked the black man, "What did Jesus say to you?" The black man responded, "Jesus said to tell you that you're a no-good pastor," and he walked out.

At eighty-four years old, Nelson still had a good sense of humor.

2: MARTIN

The next morning, I woke up surprisingly rested, and then I remembered that Alabama is in the Central Time Zone, which is an hour behind the East Coast. I had unwittingly gained an extra hour of sleep. As I gathered my thoughts, sunlight was peeking through the window and I could hear birds chirping outside. Eight hours of deep sleep was exactly what I had needed to refuel, and now I was ready to go. I went downstairs to the hotel restaurant to check out the complimentary continental breakfast. The smell of the freshly baked croissants was radiant. I helped myself to some, and soon I was ready to explore the city of Montgomery.

As I headed out, it hit me that before leaving Baltimore, a friend of mine familiar with Montgomery had recommended that I stop by a popular eating house on McDonough Street named the Farmers Market Café, which had been operated by the same family since 1959. My friend said that they had the best golden French toast in Alabama. I'd already eaten, but how could I not stop by for a quick taste? One bite in, I had to agree that my friend was right that they were delicious. And then it happened: One bite of their golden French toast rapidly led to my chowing down on a host of mouthwatering breakfast delicacies. I couldn't stop; it was like trying to put the cookies back into the cookie jar. But just as the sweet pastries left my mouth watering, I found there was also a scorching fire in my belly. I couldn't help wondering: was the café segregated in the days when it was illegal for a black person to sit down in a white-owned establishment in the South simply to have breakfast in the morning?

After leaving the Farmers Market Café, I headed into the city to play tourist for a few hours until it was time to meet up with Nelson again. I wanted to walk through Montgomery in the morning hours while everything was still quiet, to taste the soul of the city. I wanted to hear the city's heartbeat before its streets were filled with busy locals going about their day. I wanted to listen to the cobblestone streets for evidence of their vibrant past.

Montgomery is a small city, so it wasn't hard to get around, and many of the monuments and historical sites I was curious about were within walking distance of the café. My first stop was the Court Square Fountain, which was in Montgomery's historical district. According to the locals, the area around the fountain was once the location of the city's bustling slave trade. A historic plaque standing near the fountain reads: "Slaves of all ages were auctioned, along with land and livestock, standing in line to be inspected. In the 1850s, able field hands brought $1,500; skilled artisans $3,000." As a black man who had always been free to make my own choices—about where to live, what work to do, who to love, and everything else—it was mindboggling to know that in that very place, men, women, and children were bargained over and sold to the highest bidder, like furniture or vegetables, with no regard for their lives as human beings, simply because of the color of their skin.

After leaving the Court Square Fountain, I walked about six blocks down Dexter Avenue to Bainbridge Street, and then to the large white steps in front of the Alabama State Capitol. This imposing building is where legislators from all over Alabama have convened for more than 150 years to create laws and govern, even before the days of the American Civil War. During the war, in fact, the building served as the first capital of the Confederate States of America.

Ironically, also on Dexter Avenue—just a block from the first capital of a government dedicated to the oppression of black people through slavery—stands the Dexter Avenue King Memorial Baptist Church, where King delivered his Sunday sermons during the six years he lived in Montgomery. This was where he developed his skill in mesmerizing listeners with his words. The church, as I walked by it, looked immaculate, as if King might still be inside, lifting minds and hearts toward God and freedom. Montgomery was like one huge virtual museum filled with timeless monuments to the past.

Later that morning, I arrived at Nelson's house on Wabash Street for my second round of Civil Rights Movement 101. As my Uber driver pulled up in front of Nelson's two-story house, I couldn't help but notice that he had the largest home, by far, on the block. His house towered over the others, suggesting to me that the Maldens were standouts and important figures in the community. The quiet, well-manicured neighborhood was mostly filled with single-family ranch homes that lined the streets. There was a car in every driveway, a dog in every yard, and a welcome mat on every doorstop.

"Good afternoon, my friend!" Nelson welcomed me joyfully as he opened the large, solid wooden front door of his home.

As I walked through the living room and then through the kitchen, I was stopped by the smell of freshly baked biscuits. I was reminded of the exquisite baking of my grandmother, who was originally from South Carolina. Cooking, baking, and incredible food are signatures of Southern culture. It's the great common denominator that connects people from different walks of life.

"Are you hungry? I can throw some fish on the stove real fast."

"I've been eating all morning."

"Come on. It will be lunchtime soon, and it'll only take a few minutes. I have some Alabama catfish here and some fresh green beans."

There was no way I could say no to the hospitality of my host and elder. There's something indescribable about the welcoming feeling you get in the South that only a traveler there can fully appreciate.

As I sat in Nelson's study eating Alabama catfish smothered in garlic and golden butter, along with the best green beans I've ever had, he began reminiscing for me again. I already knew that Nelson wasn't just a casual observer of the civil rights movement, but I now began to understand how deep his involvement was. I also learned more about his relationship with King. It was no simple barber–client relationship.

———

Michael Martin King Jr. was born on January 15, 1929, in Atlanta, Georgia, to Baptist minister Michael King Sr. and Alberta Williams King, who was a schoolteacher. Young Michael's father was so inspired by the German Protestant religious leader Martin Luther that he adopted the same name and became Martin Luther King Sr.; his son's name was also changed to Martin.

Martin was destined to be a leader and fight for the rights of others. The elder King was an important voice for civil rights in Georgia and became the head of the Atlanta chapter of the National Association for the Advancement of Colored People (NAACP). He played a crucial role in helping to rid the state of Georgia of its oppressive Jim Crow laws, which was a priority for the NAACP. Martin Luther King Sr. was also the longtime pastor of the prominent Ebenezer Baptist Church in Atlanta, where he delivered his sermons to parishioners for decades, until his death in 1984.

Nelson knew there was something special about Martin from the first time he met the reverend. After hearing him preach at Dexter

Avenue Baptist, the young barber believed that someday Rev. King would be a powerful voice in America. Over the years, they grew very fond of each other and considered each other close friends. They stayed in touch after King moved from Montgomery to Atlanta, and on King's frequent trips back to Montgomery after the move, he would visit Nelson in the barbershop, get his usual haircut, and catch up on everything under the sun.

Nelson describes King as a family man with a good heart and one of the smartest men he ever met. The public was familiar with King's serious side, but Nelson was privileged to see his relaxed personality and good sense of humor, which he would use to joke around with people he knew well. "He could be sarcastic sometimes, but in a funny kind of way."

Nelson was also friendly with King's wife, Coretta Scott King, although she never came to the barbershop. He describes her as an elegant and classy woman, a kind and humble person, and also a proud wife who was the backbone and matriarch of the family. Nelson says that Mrs. King spent a considerable amount of time nurturing the King children. He remembers that he often saw their oldest daughter and son at church services, and that they would come into the barber-shop with their father periodically.

Martin and Coretta Scott were married on June 18, 1953, in Mar-ion, Alabama, at the home of Coretta's parents. One year later, in 1954, they moved to Montgomery, and Reverend King became the pastor at Dexter Avenue Baptist. He was only twenty-five years old at the time. Years later, Dexter Avenue Baptist Church would be renamed Dexter Avenue King Memorial Baptist Church. Today, it is a National Historic Landmark. The church still conducts services in the location where King preached some of his most riveting sermons.

Rev. Dr. Martin Luther King Jr. was beloved by people across America who were unwavering supporters of his method of protest through civil disobedience. They agreed with that practice, and they also agreed that policy changes in favor of civil rights for African Americans were desperately needed. But King also had many detractors and enemies, people who wanted to end his efforts to transform the racial landscape of America. Many people even wanted to see him dead.

It's common knowledge today that the Federal Bureau of Investigation worked to undermine King and used prohibited means to do so, ranging from illegal wiretapping and unauthorized surveillance to concentrated character assassination. FBI Director J. Edgar Hoover stated in a November 18, 1964 news conference that King was, "the most notorious liar in the country." King's home, offices, and hotel rooms were frequently wiretapped, and he was constantly harassed by Hoover's agents and threatened in ways that if used today would probably send a law enforcement official to federal prison. The FBI even sent King a letter that recommended he commit suicide.

In a declassified internal Justice Department memo dated October 7, 1963 and sent to Attorney General Robert F. Kennedy, J. Edgar Hoover wrote:

> In view of the possible communist influence in the racial situation, it is requested that authority be granted to place a technical surveillance on King at his current address or at any future address to which he may move.[1]

---

1   Del Quentin Wilber, "Aspiring Agents Learn from Mistakes of FBI 'Shameful' Investigation of Martin Luther King Jr.," *Los Angeles Times*, August 11, 2016.

In 2003, that memorandum was declassified by the Justice Department. Its text wasn't totally shocking, but it was disheartening to know that the federal government had worked in such a vicious way to undermine a leader for social justice. Today, the FBI uses the encroachment on King's civil liberties by J. Edgar Hoover as part of the bureau's cultural sensitivity training at the academy in Virginia for its new agents. It's a shameful reminder of a past injustice, but it's being used today to help right a wrong and educate others.

On January 30, 1956, the will and resolve of Rev. Dr. Martin Luther King Jr. was tested in a way that no reasonable husband or father would ever want to be tested, when the lives of his wife and his young daughter came into the crosshairs of murderous white segregationists. The Montgomery Bus Boycott that was then underway—a period of more than a year in which many blacks in Montgomery declined to ride public transportation, following the arrest of Rosa Parks for refusing to give her seat to a white man—was more than just a thorn in the side of city officials and the bus company. It was also a slap in the face to the white oppressors who, before that point, were comfortable with the city ordinances that segregated buses and humiliated African Americans with unreasonable policies. King had recently become the chairman and president of the newly formed Montgomery Improvement Association, and in that position, one of his responsibilities was to work alongside other organizations to mobilize and continue the bus boycott. On the evening of January 30, 1956, King was inside the First Baptist Church on Ripley Street, speaking at a meeting about the bus boycott, when he was told that his house had been bombed. Knowing that his wife, Coretta, and his infant daughter, Yolanda, were there, he franticly rushed home. Coretta and Yolanda were not injured, but somebody could have easily been killed. The bomb blew out the windows of the house and caused significant damage to its front porch.

Standing there in the dark of night on the badly damaged front porch of his home on Jackson Street, he tried to settle the angry mob of black people who had formed. King was quoted that night as saying, "I did not start this boycott. I was asked by you to serve as your spokesman. I want it to be known the length and breadth of this land that if I am stopped, this movement will not stop."[2]

Nelson remembers that everyone was very worried for Martin and Coretta, and many people wanted to get their guns and go after the perpetrators. He says there was little doubt as to who had carried out the bombing, as a number of white people in Montgomery had been very vocal about their feelings on the bus boycott.

———

Nelson remembers seeing suspicious white figures hanging around the barbershop—a particularly unusual sight in that segregated area of Montgomery—but at the time he didn't realize that they were FBI agents. While talking with Nelson about the bureau's harassment of the iconic civil rights leader, I could see that he still felt resentment toward them. Years after their illegal surveillance and the release of the documents confirming what was suspected by many, the mistrust that the government's behavior created still lingers.

Nelson recalls that one day when King came into the barbershop around midday, two young white men were in a car parked across the street from the barbershop. On that occasion, they were dressed casually, and there appeared to be some type of antenna on the roof of the car. Nelson didn't think much of it at the time because he thought they were salesmen selling insurance in the black community. Even so, he recalls that "Martin came into the shop and got a haircut, and when he left, so did the two men in the car across the street."

---

2   Clayborne Carson, Editor, *The Autobiography of Martin Luther King, Jr.* (Warner Books, 2001), 80.

About a month later, the reverend came back to the barbershop, and this time, two middle-aged white men parked right in front of it. One of the men got out and raised the hood of the car, as though they were having a mechanical problem. But once again, when King left, they immediately closed the hood of the car and drove off. Nelson and his brothers started speculating about whether they were a security detail that had been assigned to King. It wasn't until years later, after King died, that they found out that they were FBI agents following him.

The FBI and Hoover leveled allegations against King that he was a womanizer and a communist, but these allegations never got much traction among blacks (even though they did have their intended effect on white Southerners), and Nelson found them particularly ridiculous. He knew Martin and the King family well. He had confidence in King's good character and respected his views on the world.

"It would have taken much more for me to believe anything other than the fact that Martin was a man totally committed to the plight of black people in America," Nelson says, going on to acknowledge that King had his flaws, but was also completely committed to his cause of advancing the state of his people, and was willing to die for that cause. "There aren't a lot of people in the world who would give their lives to ensure that a stranger could have a better life. That's a rare character."

———

There was a lot of tension in Montgomery in the 1960s, but there was also a deep sense of pride in the black community, which kept its members motivated and engaged. Times were hard, but many of them felt they could turn the corner on civil rights issues. Despite the violence, they were hopeful.

"Were you ever concerned about the safety of your family there in Montgomery?" I asked Nelson.

"Every day."

He continued by explaining that he was often concerned about his own safety and the safety of his family and friends, but it was also a way of life. There was a lot of racial tension all over the South at the time, and blacks were often targets of violence. The Ku Klux Klan, white segregationists, and other hate groups were frequent terrorizers. Some of the violence was random, but much of it was organized. Cross burnings and bombings throughout the South were common. Moreover, Nelson said they happened more often than people realize, because they weren't always reported in the news or to law enforcement, and that blacks in Montgomery often became aware of incidents of violence because the information was received through a network of black churches throughout the South.

Those type of things happened all the time. This was terrorism before the mainstream media began using the word "terrorism," and it was always directed at black people. We were the victims of their ire against desegregating the South.

3: AMERICA LYNCHED

Nelson's recollection of lynchings and violence against African Americans during the days of Jim Crow is still vivid in his mind. "You could know a person one day and then the next, they were gone. Later, you would hear that they were beaten up, kidnapped, or even killed by the Klan," Nelson said. When Nelson was a young man, racially motivated assaults and killings of black people were a way of life that all African Americans were keenly aware of.

The first encounter Nelson remembers having with racist Jim Crow policies was in Pensacola, Florida, in the Crescent Department Store when he was a young child. Inside the department store were designated public water fountains, one that was labeled "Whites Only" and another that was labeled "Colored Only." Nelson said that he couldn't read well when he was a little boy, and so he ran over to the water fountain that was designated for whites only to get some water, because he was thirsty. His mother ran up behind him, slapped him hard, and yelled, "Don't you ever do that again, do you hear me?"

Nelson didn't understand why his mother was so infuriated with him. He said, "She was so angry she was turning blue in the face." As he got older and began to understand the world he was living in, Nelson saw that his mother was trying to keep him out of danger. In those years, something as innocent as that could have gotten a person of color killed in the Deep South.

Not infrequently, black people in the South were killed for the most irrational reasons, and sometimes for no reason at all. Emmett Till was a fourteen-year-old African American boy from Chicago who traveled south to visit relatives. On August 28, 1955, he was kidnapped and murdered in Money, Mississippi. The story behind the lynching of Emmett Till is still one of the most recognized and talked about in American history. It was a grotesque crime, and the level of brutality inflicted upon the young teenager helped galvanize the civil rights movement, which was just beginning to gather steam.

"I first learned about Emmett Till when I was in the barbershop one day and one of my customers was talking about the incident. He said that a little boy had been lynched down in Mississippi. A short time later, black and white people all over the country were in an uproar about what happened," Nelson said.

The murder of Emmett Till was an act of cruel senseless violence, and there were cries from many people across the country for the FBI to step in and take control of the case. But those requests landed on deaf ears. FBI Director J. Edgar Hoover made the following statement:

> There has been no allegation made that the victim has been
> subjected to the deprivation of any right or privilege which is
> secured and protected by the Constitution and laws of the
> United States.[3]

Even among many white people, the director's comments created an uproar, leading to even more support for the civil rights movement. Lynching was an act of terrorism used by people who wanted to instill

---

3   Wilber, "Aspiring Agents Learn from Mistakes of FBI's 'Shameful' Investigation of Martin Luther King Jr."

fear in others. It was a tool to punish and silence those who fought for or sympathized with black Americans and the civil rights movement. The idea that a black boy's right to live was not secured by the Constitution of the United States was an affront to both common decency and common sense.

In December 2016, President Barack Obama signed the Emmett Till Unsolved Civil Rights Crimes Reauthorization Act of 2016, which provided for the reopening of unsolved civil rights cases. According to the White House, this new law authorized the Department of Justice and the FBI to support the "full accounting of all victims whose deaths or disappearances were the result of racially motivated crimes" and "hold accountable under federal and state law individuals who were perpetrators of, or accomplices in, unsolved civil rights murders and disappearances."[4]

President Obama was applauded by civil rights lawyers and activists alike for his support of and dedication to the bill. The new law was an expansion of a previously signed law of the same name, which was passed in 2007 by Congress and signed by President George W. Bush, a surprise to some because of his Southern roots.

To better understand what led to Emmett Till's murder, the continuing violence against blacks by whites, and the need to help reconcile this deep division in society, it's important to look at the historical context.

At the time of Emmett Till's murder, there was a very strict segregation code in the South, which white Southerners enforced to keep blacks, then called "negroes" or "darkies," in their place. Under these codes, white women were to be kept away from any interaction with black men. Black men were believed to have a sexual potency and lust, and it was widely feared that any social contact at all would lead to

---

4   "S.2854 - Emmett Till Unsolved Civil Rights Crimes Reauthorization Act of 2016." Introduced April 4, 2016, https://www.congress.gov/bill/114th-congress/senate-bill/2854.

a sullying of the purity of white women. Any violation of this code was met with the threat of severe retaliation, so many black people lived highly segregated, fearful lives, with some feeling helpless to do anything to protest or violate this strict code.

It was in this context that fourteen-year-old Emmett Till came from Chicago to stay with a great uncle in Tallahatchie County, Mississippi. In Chicago, he had attended a segregated elementary school, but the world was already changing up north with the Supreme Court's 1954 verdict in *Brown v. Board of Education*, which declared that segregated education for blacks was inherently unequal and therefore illegal.[5] The atmosphere in Chicago, which had seen a huge influx of black workers from the South during the Great Migration, was more respectful to African Americans than that of Southern states.

As a result, Emmett was not prepared for the degree of segregation he encountered when he arrived in Mississippi. Moreover, Emmett had a propensity for pulling pranks, and he enjoyed pushing against some of the barriers of segregation when he was home in Chicago. In an interview with *Smithsonian Magazine*, his cousin Simeon Wright recalled that Emmett loved to tell and listen to jokes. In school, he sometimes pulled the fire alarm to get out of class, thinking that was funny. "He really had no sense of danger."[6]

As a result, he disregarded the warnings of his mother, Mamie Till-Mobley, to take care in the South because of his race.[7] She had grown up in the rural South and, like Nelson's mother, she was aware of the risks there, particularly for black men. She told him to "be very careful" and to even "humble himself to the extent of getting down on his knees."[8] But soon after his arrival, Emmett nonetheless was, in

5   Jennifer Latson, "How Emmett Till's Murder Changed the World," *Time*, August 28, 2015.

6   Abby Callard, "Emmett Till's Casket Goes to the Smithsonian," *Smithsonian Magazine*, November 2009.

7   History.com Staff, "August 28, 1955: The Death of Emmett Till," This Day in History, 2017.

8   Latson, "How Emmett Till's Murder Changed the World."

effect, on a collision course with the practices of white segregationists, which resulted in his death.

The stage was set on August 24, 1955, when Emmett stood with his cousins and their friends outside a country grocery store in Money, Mississippi. As if to flout the current strict segregation standards of the South, he bragged that he had a girlfriend back in Chicago who was white. His companions, born and raised in Mississippi, didn't believe him, and they dared him to ask the white woman behind the counter in the store, Carolyn Bryant, for a date. He didn't ask her for a date, but he did go into the store and buy candy. It was later alleged that as he left, he said, "Bye, baby" to her, even that he put his arms around her.

Simeon Wright, who was present that day, reported in a *Smithsonian Magazine* interview that Emmett was in the store for less than a minute and didn't say anything to the woman or touch her. Wright said that in the span of time Emmett was in the store, there was no time for him to do so, and that because Bryant was behind the counter, Emmett certainly didn't put his arms around her, as she later claimed. Then, as Wright and Emmett left the store together, Carolyn Bryant came out and headed to her car, and all parties agree that Emmett did whistle at her. According to Wright, Emmett was trying to impress his companions, telling them: "You guys might be afraid to do something like this, but not me." He had no idea how dangerous that was, until he saw the nervous reaction of his cousin and friends.[9]

But later, Bryant elaborated on this brief exchange, claiming that he had "grabbed her, made lewd advances, and then wolf-whistled at her as he sauntered out."[10] Much later, in 2017, Bryant admitted she had lied, exaggerating what happened that fateful day to make it seem that Emmett had far overstepped the expected boundaries of relations

---

9   Callard, "Emmett Till's Casket Goes to the Smithsonian."
10   History.com Staff, "August 28, 1955: The Death of Emmett Till."

between whites and blacks. But at the time, no one thought to question her story. If a white woman claimed an African American boy was being disrespectful to her, who was anyone to believe otherwise? No matter what a black man or boy might say to counter her claims, no one in the South would believe them.

When Roy Bryant, Carolyn's husband and the store's proprietor, returned from a business trip on August 27 and his wife told him the lie of what Emmett had done to her, he called upon his brother-in-law, J. W. Milam, to help him set things straight. Early in the morning of August 28, 1955, they went to the home of Emmett's great uncle, Mose Wright. Holding a gun to show Wright they meant business, they demanded to see Emmett, and despite Wright's pleas, they pulled Emmett out of bed and led him to their car. Though it's not certain exactly what happened, they likely drove the terrified teenager around in their car and then took him to a tool shed behind Milam's residence, where they beat him so severely that his face was barely recognizable, and shot him in the head. Then, they drove him to the Tallahatchie River, presumably already dead or dying, and threw him in the water.

Three days later, Emmett's disfigured corpse was recovered, but his face was so smashed in that Simeon Wright could only identify his body by an initialed ring he wore. After that, events moved quickly, turning what might have seemed like just another murder of a black boy into a rallying cry for the civil rights movement.

Though authorities wanted to bury Emmett's body quickly, his mother, Mamie Till-Mobley, asked the authorities to send it back to Chicago. His remains were so horrifically mutilated that she opted to have a funeral with an open casket covered by a glass top, so that she could show the world what the murderers had done to her young son. Though the service was only initially written about in *Jet*, a weekly magazine geared toward an African American audience, the accompanying photo of Emmett's corpse was so shocking that soon the mainstream media wrote about the story as well, and as they say, the rest is history. The outrage was so great that it inspired civil rights leaders to use it as a rallying cry.

Meanwhile, the Southern wheels of justice rolled on as if nothing out of the ordinary had happened—and, really, nothing had. At the trial, in a segregated courthouse in Sumner, Mississippi, only a few witnesses described Emmett Till going into the store, and Wright identified the defendants as the men who took Emmett away. But the all-white jury rendered a not-guilty verdict in less than an hour because "the state had failed to prove the identity of the body."[11]

In fact, after the two killers were acquitted and no longer subject to double jeopardy, they even justified the killing in an interview with *Look* magazine as an honor killing in defense of white supremacy in the South. As Milam stated in the interview, in which neither he nor Bryant showed any remorse, he had "intended only to beat the teen," presumably to gain his submission to and acceptance of the way things were in the South. But then the pair decided to kill him, because "he showed no fear—and refused to grovel."[12]

In 1956, J. W. Milam told *Time* magazine that Emmett Till was hopeless, and that he "liked niggas in their place . . . I know how to work 'em." In this case, Emmett had decided on not showing the expected deference, so Milam had decided, "it was time a few people got put on notice." The racist stated, "As long as I live, and can do anything about it, niggas are gonna stay in their place."[13]

Though this public confession didn't result in any further charges, since the pair had already been tried and acquitted, it contributed to the feelings of outrage that swept the nation. People had already seen Emmett's mutilated corpse in the open coffin, and these brutal and ugly comments by the killers heightened their anger.

11   History.com Staff, "August 28, 1955: The Death of Emmett Till."

12   Latson, "How Emmett Till's Murder Changed the World."

13   Ibid.

At the same time, Emmett's abduction and trial had a chilling effect on his family members. Simeon Wright's mother left the night Emmett was kidnapped and went to her brother's house in Summer, Mississippi, and later on to Chicago. She was afraid and felt that there was no way she and her husband, Mose, could live in Mississippi anymore. While Mose Wright had heard of cases like Emmett's murder happening to other black people, he had never been a firsthand victim of racism and the Jim Crow system. But now the reality of the system came home for him, and as he would later say, he "didn't want no part of Mississippi anymore."[14] A few days after the verdict in the trial was issued, the rest of the family headed to Chicago too.

It's been more than sixty years, and the Emmett Till killing still resonates in America. The outrage of the not-guilty verdict, as well as the horrendous nature of the killing, is still very much with us in recent years. Emmett's name has come up in news stories about the killing of other young black boys, such as that of Trayvon Martin by a neighborhood vigilante, George Zimmerman.

The irony, of course, is that Carolyn Bryant, now in her eighties, has admitted she lied, though it is unlikely that she will be prosecuted for the crime, since the statute of limitations on her having repeated her lie to the FBI a decade ago has long run out. Thus, although her admission may have eased her own personal guilt as she approaches the end of her life, it brings no justice or closure in the Till case. As former US Attorney and current Alabama Senator Doug Jones, who successfully prosecuted members of the Ku Klux Klan for the 1963 church bombing in Birmingham that killed four young girls, observed: "It appears that time has once again robbed us of justice in the case."[15]

Bryant's lies were very damaging to the case because of the way

14   Callard, "Emmett Till's Casket Goes to the Smithsonian."

15   Jerry Mitchell, "Emmett Till's Accuser Admits She Lied. Now his family wants the truth." *USA Today*, February 9, 2017.

she embellished the brief encounter. According to her testimony, instead of Till putting money in her hand for the candy, he grabbed her hand with a strong grip and said, "How about a date, baby?" Then, when she headed to the back of the store, she claimed Till caught her by the waist and remarked: "What's the matter, baby? Can't you take it?" After that, she declared, as she struggled to break free, he said, "You needn't be afraid of me," and then reassured her he had been with white women before. In her testimony, she said she was "scared to death," after which "this other nigger came into the store and got him by the arm" and said "Come on. Let's go."[16] And then, she said, as she ran out to the door to retrieve a pistol from her sister-in-law's car, Till whistled at her.

Those were the lies that sealed Till's fate, and Bryant's admission sixty years later made little difference to the historical events that the case set in motion. There has still been no justice for Till, and the story of racial inequality and injustice in America continues and has perhaps been made even worse now by a political climate in which racial hate can be expressed and supported by various right-wing groups in America without any condemnation from the highest levels of our government.

Emmett Till's killing may have been the most controversial and publicized killing of an African American by whites, but it's part of a long, sad history. Between 1877 and 1950, nearly four thousand black men, women, and children were hanged, burned alive, shot, drowned, and beaten to death in America, according to an Equal Justice Initiative study released in February 2015. These killings not only devastated those killed and their families, but also "traumatized black people throughout the country and were largely tolerated by state and

16   Ibid.

federal officials."[17] While the search for industrial jobs in the North were one draw, the fear of lynching is described as a major factor in the Great Migration in which my grandparents participated, which led millions of African Americans to move from the rural South to cities in the North.

The report distinguishes six types of lynchings: those that resulted from a greatly distorted fear of interracial sex; those that were a response to casual social transgressions; those that were a reaction to allegations of a serious violent crime; public spectacle lynchings; lynchings that led to large-scale violence against the whole African American community; and lynchings of community leaders, including ministers and sharecroppers, who resisted the mistreatment.

It is shocking to read about some of the practices that were widely accepted and popularized under Jim Crow laws and norms, despite their obvious barbarity. The public spectacle of a lynching drew large crowds, sometimes thousands of spectators, and the organizers often turned these into a kind of circus, where everything from postcards to body parts were sold as mementos.

The brutality of these lynchings was often extended by the prolonged torture the victim might endure before ultimately being killed, as in 1904, when Luther Holbert and his wife, whose name has been lost to history since the media who covered the story did not print it, were accused of killing a wealthy white planter in Mississippi. Before they were finally killed, both victims were tied to a tree, and their fingers and then their ears were cut off, after which Holbert was beaten so severely "that his skull was fractured and one of his eyes was left hanging from its socket." Then, after chunks of flesh were pulled from the victim's bodies, they were both thrown into a fire and burned. Meanwhile, as if it was a picnic, the white men, women, and children present enjoyed eggs, lemonade, and whiskey.[18]

---

17   Tom Mackaman, "Nearly 4,000 Blacks Were Lynched in Jim Crow South, Report Finds," World Socialist Website, February 17, 2015.

18   Mackaman, "Nearly 4,000 Blacks Were Lynched in Jim Crow South, Report Finds."

Although lynchings occurred throughout the United States, the clear majority of them occurred in the Southern states and the ones that border them—nine-tenths of them in the South, and over two-thirds of the remaining 10 percent in the six border states. Mississippi, where Emmett Till was murdered, has the grisly honor of having seen more lynchings than any other state.[19] The most common reasons from 1882 to 1951 were as the consequence of accusations of felonious assault, followed by accusations of rape or attempted rape.[20]

It's estimated that a third of the victims lynched were falsely accused of a crime.[21] Even so, the mere charge was enough to inspire whites, whether in small groups or large vigilante mobs, to take action. For the most part, these lynchings occurred in the smaller towns and isolated rural communities in the South, where people were poor and mostly illiterate and there was "a noticeable lack of wholesome community recreation."[22] In such areas, a lynching's appeal included its ability to break up the monotony of rural life, both for whites who participated and those who only watched, instigated by the entrenched racial antagonism against black Americans. Lynchings became a kind of local amusement, as well as a chance to express resentments.

In some cases, this racial violence was directed not only against a single individual, but also against an entire black community. According to Robert A. Gibson of the Yale-New Haven Teachers Institute, these riots were "the product of white society's desire to maintain its superiority over blacks, vent its frustrations in times of distress, and

19   Ibid.
20   Robert A. Gibson, *The Negro Holocaust: Lynching and Race Riots in the United States, 1890-1950.* New Haven, CT: Yale-New Haven Teachers Institute.
21   Ibid.
22   Ibid.

attack those least able to defend themselves."[23] In these riots, white mobs charged into black neighborhoods, beat and killed many blacks, and destroyed black-owned property.

In response to this white mob violence, African Americans resisted in three main ways: by retaliatory violence, by migrating to the North, and by organizing nonviolent protests. It was this last form of resistance that drove the civil rights movement. Black leaders thought that through organized nonviolent protest, they could educate the public about the horrors of lynching and get the federal government to pass anti-lynching legislation; these were the most effective ways to combat anti-black mob violence. But the struggle to make these vicious acts a federal crime was long and often futile, though the struggle against lynching did help to gradually reduce the number that were committed in the United States each year.[24]

23　Ibid.

24　Ibid.

4: BLOODY SUNDAY

"The dark sunglasses concealed his eyes, but everyone could still feel his terrorizing glare," one woman said to Nelson, and her description continued vividly. The trooper's shoes were glowing jet black from what seemed to be a recent spit shine. His uniform was clean and crisp, with sharply ironed creases in both pant legs, and the back-fill lettering on his custom-made badge was easily decipherable. He had a wide, athletic build and stood well over six feet tall, towering over most of the people in the street that day. He spat tobacco from his mouth every few minutes or so, leaving a stain on the pavement near where he stood. The description relayed was of a soldier of fortune in an army of commandos preparing to battle the common folk; yet, while the broad shoulders of the Alabama State Trooper who was blocking the roadway were threatening, the marchers would not be dissuaded.

It was March 7, 1965, and Major John Cloud and other law enforcement officials were lined up, creating a barrier like a citadel, prepared to defend what they saw as their nation's freedom—a freedom, they felt, that shouldn't belong to people of color. Cloud ordered the protesters, courageous and nonviolent men and women, to discontinue the march and disband immediately. The procession of nearly six hundred marchers refused the officer's demand and prepared to move forward. They were heading east out of Selma, planning to march fifty-four miles from Selma to the Alabama state capital of Montgomery, and had just topped the graceful arch of the Edmund Pettus Bridge, over the Alabama River, when they saw the phalanx of state and local lawmen blocking their way forward on US Highway 80.

The police stopped the marchers—led by Hosea Williams of the SCLC, and John Lewis, chairman of the Student Nonviolent Coordinating Committee (SNCC)—and ordered them to disperse. Then, quickly, the police attacked, rushing the crowd. It was violent, brutal, and swift. They cracked their whips and swung nightsticks at any person of color they could reach. They unleashed tear gas, burning the eyes of the protestors. Lewis, one of fifty-eight people injured, suffered a skull fracture. Amelia Boynton Robinson, then fifty-three years old, was beaten unconscious and left for dead, her face doused with tear gas.[25] Seventeen people would later be hospitalized.

At the direction of Alabama's governor, George Wallace, Sheriff Jim Clark of Dallas County, where Selma is located, had been told to stop the protesters from marching at any cost. In response, Clark had asked that all white males living in Dallas County be deputized in support of his effort to stop the marchers. The governor's philosophy that black people had few to no rights was on display there in Selma. The marchers weren't a group of unruly protestors refusing the orders of law enforcement officials; they were American citizens exercising their constitutional right when merciless violence was leveled against them. The attitude of the white supremacists on the Edmund Pettus Bridge that day was, "You submit, or we will break you."

But their plan didn't work exactly as Governor Wallace and Sheriff Clark had hoped. The callous attack was televised into the homes of millions of people across America, and viewers were horrified, watching

---

25   Marty Roney, "'Bloody Sunday' Altered History of a Horrified Nation," *USA Today*, March 3, 2015.

in disbelief. The events of the day showcased how white supremacists, racists, and bigots were working under the guise of segregation laws to secure their superior position, fighting an America filled with people who knew better. In the weeks that followed, the images of unarmed protesters being bludgeoned in Alabama circulated around the world.

Alabama law enforcement claimed that they were doing their job by breaking up the march, but the march would never have happened if Alabama's officers had complied with the rule of law in the first place. The Civil Rights Act of 1964, enacted just eight months prior, on July 2, 1964, outlawed discrimination based on race and prohibited unequal application of voter registration requirements. The march was in protest to the fierce resistance in Alabama, and other Southern states, faced by civil rights organizations such as the SCLC and the SNCC who attempted to help register black voters.[26] In early 1965, Martin Luther King Jr. and the SCLC had decided to make Selma, located in Dallas County, Alabama, the focus of a voter registration campaign, but Governor George Wallace and Sheriff Jim Clark led a steadfast opposition to black voter registration drives and only 2 percent of Selma's eligible black voters, three hundred out of fifteen thousand, had managed to register.[27]

The march also followed the rising racial tensions that had boiled over into bloodshed in the nearby town of Marion on February 18, 1965, when state troopers clubbed protestors, who were demanding their right to register to vote as part of a five hundred-person protest. During the attack, the troopers fatally shot twenty-six-year-old Jimmie Lee Jackson, an African American demonstrator trying to protect his mother, who was being struck by police.[28] According to Nelson:

---

26   History.com Staff, "Selma to Montgomery March," A&E Networks, 2010.

27   Ibid.

28   Christopher Klein, "Remembering Selma's 'Bloody Sunday'," History Channel, March 6, 2015.

*The marches in Selma were never supposed to happen the way they did.
It wasn't until Alabama State Troopers shot and killed that boy, Jimmie
Lee Jackson, in Marion, that everything changed. The original march
that was planned was supposed to be much smaller, but after Jimmie Lee
was shot and killed, [SCLC leader] James Bevel decided that they would
instead march for fifty-four miles from Selma to the Alabama State
Capitol in Montgomery, and so that's how the new agenda was hatched.*

———

In the same way that people remember where they were when they
heard about the attacks on America on September 11, 2001, Nelson
remembers when he first heard about the violence of Bloody Sunday.
He and his wife, Dee, had just returned home from church, around
three or four o'clock in the afternoon. "I heard about it on the radio,"
he says. "The way they beat those people was a damn shame."

*The newsman said that black demonstrators were beaten badly in
Selma. And of course, later, they showed the footage on television of the
horses trampling over people and all the gas. That's when I said that
it's going to be a pretty bad day for authorities in Selma, but I still
had no idea that it was going to be a major turning point in the civil
rights movement.*

*After Bloody Sunday happened, millions of people across America saw
the footage of the incident on television later that night. Almost everyone
in America who had a television saw the brutal violence and viciousness
of the attack by law enforcement. Those TV cameras and newsmen being
there that day had a bigger impact than anyone could have imagined at*

the time. The brutality of the beatings that were televised into people's living rooms had a lasting impact on support for segregation and policies denying people access to voting. Pictures are worth a thousand words, and seeing the beatings was much different than reading about them in the newspaper.

"Were you surprised by the reaction of white people to those images?" I asked.

Well, yes, I was. When they saw the pictures, many of them took the position that, regardless of how racist Southerners were, we can't have this in America. Bloody Sunday went far beyond just racism and segregation. The pictures were emotional, and they showed blatant disregard for human life. When I saw women being hit upside the head with clubs, I felt a cold chill, and my wife started crying. That was an ugly day for America. When I look back at how those horses trampled over people right here in America, and women were being violently attacked, we shouldn't have been surprised at how President Johnson responded. He couldn't have done anything else besides give the marchers the protection they needed during the next marches. They were lucky that no one was killed that day.

In the marches that followed, there were just as many white people participating as there were blacks, and they travelled from across the country to get to Alabama to support the protesters. That dynamic also changed the way in which Governor Wallace could respond. What was he going to do, send out more state troopers, this time to beat white people? There was no way he was going to do that. The funny thing about the whole situation was that the sheriff, Jim Clark, initially believed that he did a good job, because he did stop the marchers. But he didn't realize that the entire country would eventually see it on television. He didn't realize that seventy million people would ultimately see him and his deputies splitting the heads of women and old men.

"Didn't he see the news cameras and reporters there that day?"

Yes, but he totally underestimated how white folks around the country would react to what he was doing. Governor Wallace said to him, "Damn it, you done messed us up now!" Governor George Wallace was like the evil cartoon character that was always chasing the rabbit but could never catch him. They were such racists that it blinded them and they couldn't see straight.

Many of the protesters later that day described to Nelson how the beatings marked one of the scariest moments of their lives. His friends and clients told him that they believed they were going to die on the bridge and never see their families again.

On March 9, 1965, Martin Luther King Jr. led another march to the Edmund Pettus Bridge. About two thousand people, more than half of them white and about a third members of the clergy, participated in the second march. King led the march to the bridge and then told the protesters to disperse, knowing they had neither official permission nor protection to go further. This march became known as "Turnaround Tuesday."[29]

29   Rick Harmon, "Timeline–The Selma-to-Montgomery Marches," *USA Today*, March 5, 2015.

I still believe that the best thing Martin could have done that day was turn around and head back to the church with those people. They had no protection that day, and if someone would have gotten badly injured, like on Bloody Sunday, or even killed, that would have been a major problem for him. The day before that attempt to march to Montgomery, lawyers for the movement went in front of a federal judge in the state capital, and the judge told them that he would not approve their march and that they would have to wait for a formal hearing. Martin was aware of the judge's ruling when he attempted the march with those two thousand people, and if something bad would have happened it could have been disastrous.

Turnaround Tuesday was also covered by the media, particularly because of the quantity of people that turned out for it, but it was the violence of Bloody Sunday that prompted President Lyndon B. Johnson to take action. He understood that the images of protesters being savagely beaten by lawmen were dangerous for the nation's stability. His concern, and the concern of many legislators in Washington, was that the footage could antagonize the already contentious relationship between the government and the African American community.

On March 15, 1965, a rare joint session of Congress was convened and televised to the world. During that session, President Johnson introduced the bill that became the Voting Rights Act, which he had been working to assemble even before the attack in Selma. He gave a speech to the assembled congressmen, and to all of America, with the intention of reinforcing his support for voting rights for African Americans.

"I speak tonight for the dignity of man and the destiny of democracy," President Johnson declared. "There is no negro problem. There is no Southern problem. There is no Northern problem. There is only an American problem."[30]

On March 21, 1965, with the official permission of a federal court and the backing of the White House, a five-day-long march began. Close to eight thousand people—black and white, men and women—assembled and two thousand of them began marching the fifty-four-mile trek from Selma to Montgomery (although for safety, Johnson ordered that only three hundred people could march along the highway). Most of the marchers walked about ten miles a day and rested along Highway 80 before eventually making it to Montgomery. The march was under the protection of the Alabama National Guard, which had been called for by President Johnson. Previously, Johnson had, in telephone calls recorded by the White House, told Governor Wallace to call on the Alabama National Guard to maintain order during the march and Wallace had agreed to do so, but only hours later Wallace went on television and demanded that Johnson send in federal troops instead. Furious, Johnson told Attorney General Nicholas Katzenbach to write a press release stating that because Wallace refused to use the ten thousand available guardsmen in Alabama to preserve order in his state, Johnson himself was calling up the guard, telling them maintain order and offering all necessary support.

None of the white-owned hotels in Montgomery would lodge any of the black marchers, who needed a place to bathe and eat. So black families living in Montgomery opened their homes to strangers to provide them with a place to rest and recover after their long journey. Most of them were exhausted, and some were sick or had developed foot ailments from walking so far. Some needed medical attention. The black community of Montgomery was galvanized because they understood how important that moment in time was.

---

30   Cydney Adams, "March 15, 1965: LBJ speaks before Congress on Voting Rights," CBS News, March 15, 2016.

On March 24, the marchers began to slowly arrive at the staging area on the outskirts of Montgomery. Nelson was there that evening, waiting as the marchers sporadically trickled in following their long, grueling, and dangerous journey. They rested at the City of St. Jude, a Catholic Church and school complex, where Harry Belafonte, Tony Bennett, Joan Baez, Sammy Davis Jr., Nina Simone, Frankie Laine, and Peter, Paul, and Mary performed at a "Stars for Freedom" rally.[31]

I asked Nelson if there was any violence from the KKK or any of the other hate groups and he said, "The marchers had the National Guard protecting them on Highway 80, but they needed to be covered for more than fifty miles."

> *The violence wasn't to the level of what was expected. People were afraid for their lives, but they still chose to participate. The presence of the Guard as well as the FBI made a difference, but there was still some violence, and there was one person who was killed on the final day of the marches. Ironically, she was a white woman. The Klan shot her in the head.*

Viola Fauver Gregg Liuzzo was a thirty-four-year-old white woman from Detroit, Michigan, who was also a committed civil rights activist. She had travelled to Alabama to support the marchers after seeing King's plea on television asking that people from across the country come to Selma. Viola was killed on the night of March 25, 1965. That night, she was driving another civil rights worker with the SCLC—an African American teenager named Leroy Moton—back to Selma on Highway 80 when another car pulled alongside her vehicle. One of the passengers in the neighboring car shot Liuzzo, striking her in the face and killing her. Her car ended up in a ditch, and Moton survived the attack by pretending to be dead.

---

31   Harmon, "Timeline–The Selma to Montgomery Marches."

The following day, President Johnson appeared on television to announce that Liuzzo's killers had been caught. The police arrested four members of the Ku Klux Klan for the killing: Eugene Thomas, Collie Leroy Wilkins Jr., William O. Eaton, and Gary Thomas Rowe.[32] A few weeks later, the trial of Collie Leroy Wilkins (alleged by the prosecution to be the triggerman in Liuzzo's murder) began in Hayneville, Alabama. Defense attorney Matthew Hobson Murphy Jr., Imperial Klonsel of the United Klans of America, informed the jury that since Rowe had broken his Klan loyalty oath by testifying against his fellow klansmen, they should not believe anything he said, and asserted that Liuzzo was a white woman alone in a car with a black man at night and so whatever happened to her was her own fault. Murphy was successful in his attempts to blame Liuzzo for her own fate, and the trial ended in a hung jury.[33] A second Alabama jury cleared Wilkins of all charges, and none of the klansmen was ever convicted of murder. Wilkins and Thomas did, however, each serve seven years out of a ten-year sentence for federal charges of conspiracy to violate Liuzzo's civil rights. Eaton died before his sentence began.

On March 25, the march culminated with Rev. Dr. Martin Luther King Jr. leading the supporters through the streets of Montgomery—where Rosa Parks, a decade earlier, had refused to give up her seat on the bus and where schools were segregated until 1954—to the steps of the Alabama State Capitol. Fifty thousand supporters met the marchers in Montgomery and gathered in front of the Alabama State Capitol to hear King speak.[34] There on the steps of the statehouse, thousands of people from all walks of life prayed together, cried together, and celebrated together, honoring a well-fought and historic victory.

32   Biography.com Editors, "Viola Gregg Liuzzo Biography," A&E Television Network, February 19, 2016.

33   Mary Stanton, *From Selma to Sorrow: The Life and Death of Viola Liuzzo*, Athens: University of Georgia Press, 1998.

34   History.com Staff, "LBJ Sends Federal Troops to Alabama," This Day in History, March 20, 1965.

Nelson was on the steps of the Alabama State Capitol on March 25, 1965, standing with Nobel Peace Prize winner Ralph Bunche, and just a few feet away from King as he addressed the crowd that day with his "How Long, Not Long" speech. Ralph Bunche was the first African American to receive the Nobel Peace Prize, fourteen years before King did. "He was a very accomplished and prominent colored man," Nelson said, describing Bunche. "He was a negotiator and he was involved in brokering a peace deal between the Arabs and Israel in the Middle East." Bunche did this as part of the various tasks he performed on behalf of the United Nations. He was also a close friend and advisor to King and helped develop civil rights strategies. In 1963, he was awarded the Presidential Medal for Freedom by President John F. Kennedy.

After speaking with Nelson for many months about the American civil rights movement and the people and events that played major roles in its success, I increasingly felt that in school, and in life, I had missed out on some of the most important parts of American history. I would have loved to have been in Selma with the people who were making a difference. I was grateful to be able to see through Nelson's stories the events that unfolded in front of his eyes and to hear about the character of the people leading the movement. This was a unique opportunity.

5: THE COLORED WAITING ROOM

My first visit to the Deep South was everything I expected it to be and more. Sometimes it was so painful that it was hard for me to wrap my mind around what I was hearing. There were moments while I was listening to Nelson's stories that I felt intense anger toward whites. There were other times when I felt as if I had gone through a time machine and arrived fifty years in the past, in the middle of the racial strife and segregation. There were also times when I felt anxious, as if Ku Klux Klan members might drive up beside me at any time in an old pickup truck, waving a Confederate flag and yelling, "Nigger, go back to Baltimore!"

When I think about how an entire race of people was mistreated so horrifically and for so long only because of the color of their skin, it's a hard pill for me to swallow. It's tough when you think about how a black person wasn't allowed to enter a lunch counter, diner, or café in the South, and that there were even public bathrooms labeled "Whites Only." There were moments in Montgomery when my emotions were all over the place. Sometimes I didn't know what to feel, and other times I was embarrassed that I was American.

In the summer of 2017, I decided to return to Montgomery to see Nelson, but this time I wanted to visit Selma too. I had an urge to take a walk backward through history there, across the Edmund Pettus Bridge, the site of the Bloody Sunday attacks. I wanted to stand in the spot where the protesters had bled in 1965 and try to imagine that emotional day. I wanted to put my feet on the same ground where thousands of people had once made a tremendous sacrifice to support freedom and justice.

So there I was, on my way to the airport in Baltimore in the early morning again, ready to pile up more frequent flier miles and journey back into the Deep South. It took me two hours to get to Harts-field-Jackson International Airport in Atlanta, and from there I rented a car and drove to Selma. The drive was another two hours, and my mind raced the whole time. What would it feel like when I arrived? Would I feel a connection to the people who'd marched? Would I feel a stronger connection to my African American identity? Would I feel anything?

After I reached Montgomery, I veered onto US Highway 80 and from there it was a straight shot to Selma. As I drove, I kept thinking of the regular people, like myself, who travelled the same road in their march for civil rights. Many of them were teachers, janitors, or wait-ers, others were doctors or students, and they came from all over the country. The majority were young activists.

I arrived at Edmund Pettus Bridge in Selma around ten-thirty a.m., drove over the bridge and the Alabama River, and parked the car on Water Avenue. I felt excited, happy, overwhelmed, and disgusted all at once. There was a plethora of emotions tangled together in my head, and my heart was beating rapidly.

I stepped slowly out of the car, and as soon as my feet hit the ground, I felt an odd energy shoot through me. Instantly, my legs were weak and my soul was weary. I thought of the pain that a young John Lewis must have felt during the vicious attack that almost killed him there in 1965. I also thought of the photos of Amelia Boynton lying on the ground after being knocked unconscious.

The crude steel beams that supported the seventy-nine-year-old bridge were strong, sturdy, and intimidating. As I walked along it, I looked down at the asphalt that had been stained fifty years ago with the blood of black men and women. Those stains were no longer visible, but I could see them in my mind, and I could hear the desperate screams of innocent people as the mounted deputies rushed the demonstrators. In the pit of my stomach I could feel the agony of the men who suffered broken bones and the women who were trampled that day. I could hear the voices of the Alabama State Troopers who were pleased by what they accomplished. I began to wonder if those who had inflicted pain that day in Selma were ever remorseful for their ugly deeds—or if any of them was still alive and remembering that day with satisfaction and glee. The latter thought made my stomach churn. Fifty years seemed like a long time ago and no time at all.

If I could have cried I would have, but the tears wouldn't flow. They were obstructed by anger and resentment. It pained me to know that people were brutally assaulted that day and that the perpetrators never faced justice. I knew that the injured had physical scars and I thought about all the people who probably had psychological scars too.

After spending an hour in deep thought on the Edmund Pettus Bridge, looking out onto the muddy waters of the Alabama River, I was mentally drained. It was like the muddy brown waters of the river stood in for the blood that had been shed. I walked back down the bridge toward my car and read the plaque that had been placed at the foot of the bridge to memorialize the Selma marches. That's when I spotted a small restaurant on Water Avenue named Charlie's Place. I was hungry and wanted to rest, and after the morning I'd had, I thought that I deserved a good Southern meal.

When I walked into Charlie's Place, there was a white waitress with a warm smile standing at the front counter greeting customers. Posted on a twelve-foot-high chalkboard was the restaurant's mouthwatering menu, a mix of salads, seafood, and greasy burgers made to your liking. My choice for lunch was easy that day: two crab cakes, fried green tomatoes, and one tall glass of lemonade. As I sat waiting for my food to arrive, I realized again how surreal my trip to Selma was. During the period when the Selma marches were taking place, over fifty years before, white-owned restaurants in Selma were still overtly segregated. They probably would have had a serious problem with a black man from Baltimore sitting there eating a meal.

———

The drive from Selma back to Montgomery was a straight shot down a desolate Highway 80. Along the fifty-four-mile stretch of highway there were a handful of antiquated gas stations, cow pastures, and farms, but otherwise there wasn't much real estate in between the two historic Alabama cities. Other than a few tractor trailers hauling undisclosed loads, and a few UPS trucks, there weren't many vehicles on the road either.

When I arrived back in Montgomery, it was only late afternoon, but it seemed as if the city was abandoned; it looked like a ghost town. I assumed that it was because the students from Alabama State and Troy State University's satellite campus were still out of school for the summer break. Then I thought that maybe it was deserted because the state legislators, who were usually there in the capital rubbing elbows with lobbyists, were also on vacation. The legislative session for the year had ended a few months earlier, and the capital was silent.

I had just walked into the lobby of my hotel after the drive from Selma when I received a call from Nelson.

"Hey, Kevin, are you here yet? Can you meet me at the barbershop around three?"

When the traffic light changed, I proceeded across High Street onto the 400 block of S. Jackson Street and there it was: number 407, the acclaimed Malden Brothers Barbershop, born in 1958 by three brothers, all born during the days of Jim Crow and segregation in the South.

Today the barbershop has a new owner. Nelson passed the torch in 2017 to a young man who had previously worked in the shop. He had started out sweeping its floors and now he's a proud entrepreneur and businessman.

It was a hot and humid day in Centennial Hill when I arrived, just like it was on my first visit. The neighborhood kids were out riding bicycles and running up and down the block, enjoying the summer heat. Montgomery neighbors were sitting outside, on the porches of their homes, looking content with life. As I parked the car and stepped out, I noticed what looked like a college fraternity house near the corner. I assumed the people who lived there were students at Alabama State University, which was just a few blocks up the street. The area seemed to be a low- to middle-income neighborhood in need of some redevelopment. Almost sixty years ago, when the neighborhood was vibrant and alive, it probably looked a lot different.

The outside of the barbershop is nondescript, and if you're driving and not paying attention, you can easily miss it. Even when you notice it, it looks like many of the others that you would see tucked away in black communities across the United States. The front door of the shop was old and worn. The visual key to the magic that took place inside was the weathered wooden bench sitting in front of the barbershop with the name "MALDEN BROTHERS" painted in block letters.

As I turned the doorknob and slowly pushed the door open, it made a harsh screeching sound. I walked inside and felt as if I had walked into a museum filled with treasures from the past. The walls inside the barbershop were plastered with hundreds of photos of people who played significant roles in the civil rights movement and the years that followed. Hanging on the wall was a powerful photo of Coretta Scott King standing in front of a podium, addressing an audience. There was another photo of the young civil rights activist Julian Bond in Selma, marching with other proud people to the Alabama State Capitol. And there was a portrait photo of Rev. Dr. Martin Luther King Jr. from when he became the pastor of Dexter Avenue Baptist Church, in 1954. There was also a photo of General Daniel "Chappie" James Jr., who was the first African American four-star general in the United States Military. When Nelson was a child in Pensacola, Florida, he attended a private school operated by the general's mother, Lillie James.

"So here is where it all began, in 1958," Nelson said as he stood behind one of the barber chairs.

This was my chair, where King sat to get his hair cut every two weeks or so. Here in the middle barber's chair was where my brother Stephen sat his clients. He was a barber from 1958 until the time he retired and went back to Pensacola, in 1993. And this last chair is where my other brother, Spurgeon, cut hair. We spent most of our lives right here in this barbershop. Spurgeon died in 1995 from cirrhosis of the liver. He really liked to drink a lot, and eventually it caught up with him in the worst way. That was a sad time.

As I stood scanning the room filled with old pictures and remnants from the past, a large, menacing sign hanging from the ceiling near the back of the room grabbed my attention. The sign read: "THE COLORED WAITING ROOM."

This was the first time I ever saw an original sign with this message up close, and in the barbershop, with Nelson, the impact hit hard, and the anger and embarrassment came quickly. *How could my country have once thought that segregation was a good public policy for its citizens?*

Nelson explained that the sign was given to him years ago by a collector who picked it up in St. Louis, Missouri. The sign was authentic and was originally posted inside a rail station in St. Louis, to identify the area where blacks were permitted to wait for trains. As in Montgomery, public transportation in St. Louis was segregated for decades. "Wherever this sign stood, that's where you stood if you were black. If you stood or hung around anywhere else in the station, you could be arrested or even assaulted by a mob of whites."

Those were the conditions that we had to contend with in Southern states during those years. You often hear people saying that we've come a long way, but the problem with that statement is that the heads of white America were buried so deep in the sand that we're still just scratching the surface today.

There was a smaller sign hanging from the ceiling in the barbershop that read, "KIDNAPPER AND SLAVE CATCHER: Keep A Sharp Look Out for Kidnappers and Have a Top Eye Out!" The sign was printed with the date "April 24, 1851." It was a warning sign notifying blacks that kidnappers and slave catchers were in the area. A slave catcher was a person hired to track down escaped slaves, before slavery was abolished with the ratification of the Thirteenth Amendment in 1865. The slave catchers would return slaves to their owners, and the returned slaves would be beaten savagely, often killed.

Standing in the barbershop, the two signs were so close to me that I could reach out and touch them. People instinctively want to distance themselves from bad things, and it's easy for the mind to shelve photos from history books in the same place it puts storybook photos, but here was physical proof that the photos I'd seen were real.

I paused to process the signs and then I turned to a more uplifting subject. "Is that Congressman John Lewis?" I asked while pointing at one of the many pictures on the wall.

"Yes."

"He looks really young in this picture. How old is he now?"

"I don't know. Close to eighty, I guess."

"He's been around a long time."

"A few months ago, he stopped by to say hello. He was in town for an event with Congresswoman Terri Sewell, who represents the congressional district down in the Black Belt. John was one of the key figures among the Freedom Riders. He's lucky to be alive today. He put his life on the line many times for the movement. When he was younger, he received a few severe beatings from those white boys, and he was probably arrested thirty or forty times."

John Lewis was only a young man during the years of the civil rights movement, but he was one of the leaders of the SNCC long before becoming a Georgia congressman. SNCC was comprised of young black and white college students and supporters. Nelson said they worked on several projects during the civil rights movement, projects such as the Freedom Rides of 1961, in which busloads of black and white students rode into segregated areas of the South where segregation in bus terminals was still being practiced, regardless of its illegality, and the Mississippi Freedom Summer of 1964, which focused on increasing voter registration among African Americans in Mississippi who had been obstructed from voting for decades. Many people were injured in both events after being attacked by the Ku Klux Klan. James Chaney, Andrew Goodman, and Mickey Schwerner were killed during the Freedom Summer.

"It was tough being black in America then, but it was even tougher being a black leader in America. Instantly you became a target and you were constantly under attack," Nelson said.

I told Nelson that I'd seen a YouTube video of John Lewis being beaten by state troopers on Bloody Sunday during the marches in Selma. He received a concussion.

They almost killed him here in Montgomery during one of those bus rides. He had a lot of courage, and, like I said, he put his life on the line on many occasions during the movement, which earned him respect. He was one of the speakers in DC during the 1963 March on Washington. He was standing right there next to Reverend King and Ralph Abernathy.

When they were busing those students down into Mississippi to protest, they encountered a lot of violence there. The Klan put up a lot of resistance because they didn't want to have anything to do with desegregation. Segregation was a practice that they enjoyed and benefitted from, and anything other than that was unacceptable to them.

"Were there any places that weren't segregated?"

"No. Everything was segregated until President Johnson passed the 1964 Civil Rights Act. The churches were segregated, the schools, restaurants, even the beaches were segregated. Even after the law was passed, enforcement was an issue."

"The beaches?"

Yes. Even the beaches were segregated. I left Pensacola, Florida, when I was eighteen years old, but when I was still a kid living there, I went to the beach frequently. During that time, there was Pensacola Beach, which was only for white people, and there was Johnson Beach, which was for black people. The white folks stayed on their beach, and we stayed on the black beach. Wait a minute! There was one more place back then where blacks could swim, and it was Wingate Beach. A black man owned the land, which was on the Gulf, and from time to time, me and my friends would go swimming there too. It was a beautiful place with white sand. I would go there sometimes with my parents.

If you were to step foot on the segregated white beach, you would be arrested because segregation was the law of the land. There was no race mixing in public places in those years. And if you weren't arrested, you would probably be attacked and jumped on by white boys.

Desegregating the South was a painstaking process for federal officials in Washington, DC. Segregation policies and laws were firmly embedded in the South, and it had been that way for almost a century after the abolition of slavery. On June 11, 1963, Governor George Wallace stood at the door of the University of Alabama's Foster Auditorium with local law enforcement officials, attempting to block the entrance of Vivian Malone and James Hood, two black students who were attempting to complete their college class registration on campus.[35] The incident became known as the "Stand in the Schoolhouse Door," and it symbolized the struggle to end oppression in the South.

Nelson had a photo of the incident hanging on the wall in the barbershop, in immaculate condition. The image was a reminder of the hard-fought struggle to desegregate and the resistance of powerful men like Governor Wallace, who may have been the most powerful and feared racist in the South in the 1960s.

Over the eighty-four years that Nelson has lived in the South, he's met thousands of white men who've possessed the same ideology on

---

35   Debra Bell, "George Wallace Stood in the Doorway at the University of Alabama 50 Years Ago Today," *US News & World Report*, June 11, 2013.

race relations as Governor Wallace. They were bigots and racists who believed that the practice of segregation was rational and critical, and they were even willing to kill to maintain it. George Wallace was the poster child for Jim Crow policies in the South. His supporters were white supremacists who believed in the outlandish 1857 Supreme Court ruling in the Dred Scott decision that took the legal position that black people in American were "subordinate, inferior beings— whether slave or freedmen."

I told Nelson that I often hear my peers making statements critical of African Americans who lived during the civil rights era. "Their criticism is often about how many of the people who participated in the protests didn't physically fight back against the police. I still cringe sometimes when I see the footage of black students being violently sprayed with a fire hose and pelted in the face and head with food and ketchup in Birmingham and Greensboro during the protest sit-ins at lunch counters."

"That's partially where some of the disconnect and lack of under-standing lies between the generations about that era," said Nelson.

There's a lot that your generation doesn't understand about the civil rights movement. Reverend King's entire message was about nonviolent protests and demonstrations. He adopted that philosophy from Mahatma Gandhi. Nonviolent protests were unique in the sense that it required self-restraint and discipline to participate in them. If an individual didn't have self-control, that could have been a major problem for everyone else involved in the protest. If one protester was to engage the police officers, state troopers, or even those crazy racist white boys in a physical altercation, a response like that could have unleashed a barrage of violence on everyone else. The goal was to protest, make your point heard, and put pressure on the government to change policy. It wasn't to get into a fistfight or a war. That was the burden that Reverend King shouldered in every demonstration and protest he participated in or that he directed. If Martin himself had struck back when he was pushed by the police, others would have undoubtedly done the same. Each time he participated in a protest, demonstration, or march, he had the safety and the lives of others in his hands, the lives of the people who believed in him.

Nelson made a point that I had never really considered. The goal of civil rights protestors wasn't to go to war with law enforcement officials, because that would have been a war they couldn't win. The bloodshed and the number of lives that would have been lost in the African American community would have been astronomical.

Look, we were born into those conditions and there was a time when some blacks didn't see anything wrong with segregation. When you're born into those circumstances, that's all you know. You don't immediately understand what desegregation means until you're educated on the issue. That's when you begin to learn that you have rights too, human rights, and that segregation laws aren't just civil rights violations—they are also human rights violations.

Those were the things that Martin and many of the other civil rights leaders in those days helped the people understand. They educated themselves and they studied the issues, then they shared what they learned with the community and they helped the people become educated. They educated common folks about their civil rights and their constitutional right to vote. They educated people on their right to be equal and their right to be treated fairly in America. Don't misunderstand me, we knew that the Jim Crow laws were oppressive, but what we had to learn was that there was something we could do about it. Educating the people about the issues was the best thing that could've

happened to the community, but the nonviolent approach we used was
also important. After educating the people on the issues, there was a plan
of action to evoke the changes we wanted to see, but nonviolent protests
were the vehicle that got us there.

———

I mentioned to Nelson that while I was driving down S. Jackson Street, I accidentally drove by King's old home.

"You mean the Parsonage? It's a museum now. That's the house he lived in while he was here in Montgomery, from 1954 until he moved back to Atlanta in 1960. The Dexter Avenue Baptist Church has always owned the property, even before he lived there, but several years after his death, they converted it into a museum people could visit."

"I didn't even know that he lived in Montgomery until I met you. I thought he lived in Atlanta."

"Well, he was born and raised in Atlanta, but he lived here for six years. Do you want to go see the house?"

"Absolutely!"

"Okay. Well, I better lock this door first. Meet me out front and follow me in your car. We could walk, but it's still a little too hot out there for me."

It took all of sixty seconds to drive from the barbershop across High Street to the Dexter Parsonage Museum. The outside of the building was well kept, and the grounds were neatly maintained. The white two-story single-family house at 309 S. Jackson Street could have blended into almost any residential landscape in America.

"All he had to do was walk one block up the street to get to the barbershop. Reverend King could literally see the shop from his front porch. He was basically a neighbor of ours. Let's go up onto the porch so that I can show you something.

"See this hole?"

Nelson was pointing at a one-foot-by-one-foot crater on the right side of the porch as you come up the steps. Next to it on the porch was a plaque that read:

During Dr. M. L. King Jr.'s pastorate of the Dexter Avenue Baptist Church, the small crater nearby marks the spot were a bomb exploded on the evening of 30 January 1956. Coretta S. King, 10-week-old Yolanda Denise and Dexter member Mary Lucy Williams, were in the house. None were hurt.

"This is where the bomb was when it exploded in 1956, when the Klan tried to blow up his house."

"Was that the first assassination attempt on his life?"

"Well, he wasn't home when the bomb went off, but I guess you can say that. The people who left the bomb probably didn't know that he wasn't home that night. Based on the damage that was done to the structure, they must have used a lot of explosives. They damn near blew off the front of the house."

"I wanted to take you inside the museum and show you around, but I forgot that today is Monday and they're closed." Nelson said. "I know what we can do! Let's go downtown before it gets too late. I'll ride with you and you can bring me back to my car after we're done."

After leaving Jackson Street, we drove about two miles to the Civil Rights Memorial Center on Washington Avenue. I was awestruck by the memorial that was inscribed with the names of the forty-one people who were murdered during the civil rights struggle between 1954 and 1968. They were memorialized in stone. This brought home to me the notion that Alabama really was the epicenter of the struggle for justice. The entire state was one big civil rights artifact.

Inside the Civil Rights Memorial Center, we found the Wall of

Tolerance, which displayed the names of thousands of people who made a commitment to labor against injustice and hate in America. After taking a pledge, visitors could sign the display digitally, and their names would instantly appear on the wall and become part of the exhibit. It was a moving reminder that the need for vigilance against injustice continues today.

After leaving, Nelson and I took the short drive down Washington Avenue to the Rosa Parks Library and Museum. The location of the museum is just a few blocks away from where Rosa Parks was arrested on December 1, 1955, while riding on the Cleveland Avenue bus. The attention her action received cemented her place in history. According to the information in the museum, she was referred to by Congress as "the first lady of civil rights." Inside of the museum was a replica of the bus on which Parks was a passenger when the bus driver, James Blake, unlawfully ordered her to give up her seat to a white male passenger. This repository of historical facts was filled with displays and exhibits from before, during, and after the civil rights era, along with breathtaking photos of the life of the iconic activist.

"Here's the exhibit that I'm a part of," Nelson said as he pointed to a wall of the museum. The exhibit was titled "Hands Uplifted for Freedom and Justice," and it displayed fifty bronze handprints, which represented unsung heroes who played various roles in the movement. The project's originator and coordinator, Janet Adams, of Montgomery, said she envisioned the exhibit to honor civil rights movement participants whose service is less widely known.[36] "For every well-known participant, there were many others whose dedication and service gave the movement its solid base," Adams had said. "These faces in the crowd joined protest organizations, spearheaded student demonstrations, attended rallies, raised their voices in song, sheltered

---

36   Troy News Center, "'Hands Uplifted' Exhibit to Honor Civil Rights Movement Participants, " March 2, 2010.

outsiders who came to offer moral support."[37]

Nelson had played a role in altering history, and he was honored in the museum in a significant way. His name was on the wall right next to one of the bronze hands that represented the unsung heroes. I could see Nelson's eyes tear up a bit as we stood there looking at the display.

As we continued my short, private tour of the first floor of the museum, Nelson directed me into a large room that housed a very dramatic exhibit, "The Fabric of Race: Racial Violence and Lynching in America." It was a visual examination of racial violence and lynching in America created by artist Renee Billingslea. The installation includes hundreds of white dress shirts, burned and stained, each with a hand-embroidered identity tag, which hang from a gallery wall to honor forgotten victims.[38] It was unnerving to see, but it was also powerful. I kept thinking, *What if a museum visitor casually reached up to read one of the tags on the shirts in the exhibit and spotted the name of a family member who had been lynched?* There are so many people whose family legacies will forever bear the scars of slavery.

After leaving the "Fabric of Race" exhibit, we walked out into the hallway, and a large photograph on the wall grabbed my attention. "Nelson, where was this picture of Mrs. Parks taken?"

"That's a picture from the March on Washington, in 1963. The men marched down Pennsylvania Avenue and the women marched down Independence Avenue."

I didn't realize that Rosa Parks was involved in the historic march in 1963—though I would have been surprised if she had not been there. She was a large figure in the civil rights movement and the March on Washington was its largest demonstration.

There were no women speakers during the main presentation of

---

37   Ibid.

38   Staff Reports, "Exhibit Examining Racial Violence, Lynching Coming to Rosa Parks Museum," *USA Today*, April 19, 2017.

the March on Washington, and this created controversy. Although black women were central to the movement for civil rights, sexism was still a societal norm. Renowned gospel singer Mahalia Jackson sang during the program, but she was the only female presenter.

"How much do you know about the March on Washington?" Nelson asked.

"I don't know much about it. That's where King gave his 'I've Been to the Mountaintop' speech, right?"

"No, no! The March on Washington was the event where Martin delivered his 'I Have a Dream' speech."

6: MARCH ON

On August 28, 1963, an estimated two hundred fifty thousand Americans gathered in Washington, DC, for the March on Washington for Jobs and Freedom, or simply, the March on Washington. The event was organized by several civil rights and religious groups and was designed to shed light on the political and social challenges that African Americans continued to face. The march culminated with Martin Luther King Jr.'s famous "I Have a Dream" speech, a spirited call for racial justice and equality, delivered on the steps of the Lincoln Memorial, in front of DC's National Mall, to both black and white Americans, and televised for audiences across the country to watch.

The demonstration sent a stern message to America and to the world: African Americans and other minorities had the power to organize, and they would use that power to evoke change. To achieve such a lofty goal, the NAACP and the SCLC put aside their long-standing rivalry; black and white groups across the country were urged to attend the march; and elaborate arrangements were made to ensure a harmonious event. The growing disillusionment among some civil rights workers after nearly a decade of agitation without sufficient federal action would have been reflected in a speech planned by John Lewis of the SNCC, but to preserve the atmosphere of goodwill, leaders of the march persuaded Lewis to omit his harshest criticisms of the Kennedy administration.[39]

Nelson remembers that he had no idea what a historic event the march would turn out to be. "I thought that it would be just another movement event orchestrated by Bayard Rustin and A. Philip Randolph. I thought that it was just going to be an event in support of poor people and a demand for more jobs. I had no idea that so many people from all over the country were going to be there."

Nelson said that in his opinion, what made the march so successful and outstanding was the number of people involved. The government had no idea that black people had the ability to organize on that level. On August 28, DC swelled with civil rights supporters from all over the United States. They drove in, bussed in, and took trains. Three student marchers walked and hitchhiked seven hundred miles to get there. Thousands of people waved signs and cheered as they listened to speakers address the civil rights problems challenging America. The last speaker was Martin Luther King Jr.[40]

> *Reverend King was invited to be one of the guest speakers, and that's clearly one of the things that helped make it so successful. The funny part was that he had no idea at that time that he was going to deliver one of the most historic speeches of the twentieth century.*

The night before the March on Washington, King asked his aides for advice about the following day's speech. "Don't use the lines about 'I have a dream,'" his adviser Wyatt Walker told him. "It's trite, it's a cliché. You've used it too many times already." King had indeed employed the refrain several times before. Just a week earlier, he had used it at a fundraiser in Chicago, and a few months before that at a

---

39   History.com Staff, "March on Washington," A&E Networks, 2009

40   "The March on Washington for Jobs and Freedom," *PBS Newshour*, August 27, 2003.

huge rally in Detroit. As with most of his speeches, both had been well received, but neither had been regarded as momentous.[41]

But while King had received advice from some of his most trusted advisors to not use the "I have a dream" part of the speech, he was being encouraged by others to do just the opposite. As he was delivering it, Mahalia Jackson, no stranger herself to the art of holding an audience riveted, whether in a church or onstage—called out to him from a short distance away.

"He was just reading, and she just shouted to him, 'Tell them about the dream, Martin! Tell them about the dream!'" said Clarence Jones, an attorney and adviser to King who had contributed to the writing of the speech. "I was standing about fifty feet behind him, to the right and to the rear, and I watched him—this is all happening in real time—just take the text of his speech and move it to the left side of the lectern, grab the lectern, and look out.[42] I said to somebody standing next to me, 'These people don't know it, but they're about ready to go to church.'"[43]

King looked out over the crowd, and as he later explained in an interview, "Suddenly, this thing came to me that I have used—I'd used many times before, that thing about 'I have a dream'—and I just felt that I wanted to use it here." King said, "I say to you today, my friends, so even though we face the difficulties of today and tomorrow, I still have a dream." And then he was off, delivering some of the most famous lines ever spoken, words that he hadn't planned to use and that some of the civil rights leaders who attended the march believed only the marchers would remember.[44]

41   "I Have A Dream Speech," *The Huffington Post*, January 8, 2011.

42   Dave Walker, "Witnesses Recall Role of New Orleans' Mahalia Jackson in Martin Luther King Speech," *The Times-Picayune*, August 23, 2013.

43   Ibid.

44   Drew Hansen, "Mahalia Jackson, and King's Improvisation," *New York Times*, August 27, 2013.

Mahalia Jackson had been with Reverend King on many occasions. She was standing not far from him, and she knew then that he wasn't at his best, so she yelled at him, "Martin, put the dream in there," because she had heard him deliver that speech in the past and knew that it would electrify the crowd. That's when Reverend King closed the book that was sitting in front of him.

Using the words that Nelson and many others described as the speech of the century, King said: "I have a dream that one day every valley shall be exalted, every hill and mountain shall be made low, the rough places will be made plain, and the crooked places will be made straight, and the glory of the Lord shall be revealed, and all flesh shall see it together."

King's "I Have a Dream" speech used words from the Bible's Book of Isaiah 40:5 and was similar in tone to the Atlanta Compromise Speech that Booker T. Washington delivered in 1895 before a predominantly white audience, which Nelson called a "nonthreatening speech."

Booker T. Washington told white people that we're going to work with you, and when your momma and daddy get sick, we're going to take care of them on their death bed, and then we're going to go to the cemetery with tears in our eyes and grieve with you. After that speech, they named every school in the United States of America after Booker T. Washington. When Reverend King gave that speech in Washington, white Americans didn't view it as frightening or threatening. The liberals and moderates were more reassured by his words, while the bigots hated him even more.

"How did blacks in Montgomery react to King's speech when they heard it?"

Well, most of them had never heard him speak like that before. But since television and radio were just beginning to become advanced and available to more blacks, in a very short time the content of his speech spread throughout the country. People across the nation were excited after hearing a black man deliver a speech like that. For about two weeks straight, Reverend King's speech on the Mall in Washington was the only topic being discussed in the barbershop. Some guys were misquoting him and everything! While one guy was saying that King said this, another guy in the shop would argue and say that Martin said something different. Some of my customers with more radical ideologies had a problem with Martin saying one day little black boys and girls will hold hands with little white boys and girls. They didn't understand the point he was trying to make in the speech about unity and bringing people together. You even had some people making the argument that the March on Washington speech wasn't his best, and that they'd heard him deliver other speeches that were just as powerful.

In the Malden Brothers Barbershop, debates over big events were the norm, whether they were sporting events, political events, or tragedies. Even King's speech, as well as the gathering of approximately two hundred fifty thousand people in the nation's capital, was not an event that everyone saw the same way.

Of course, the event wasn't perfect, Nelson said, and broached the topic of how women should have had more of a role. "One of the major mistakes that Bayard Rustin and A. Philip Randolph, the primary organizers, made was not allowing the women to have their voices heard onstage. That was a major blunder." Although women participated in the planning and execution, they were severely underrepresented and it didn't reflect well on the organizers. The wives of the leaders weren't allowed to march with their husbands, and none of the women involved were invited to meet with President Kennedy. Most of the debate over this went on behind the scenes and the march was deemed an overall success; but Nelson said, "It created unnecessary friction at a time when all blacks, men and women, needed to come together," Nelson said.

Another critic of the speech was the historian and pan-African pedagogue John Henrik Clarke, who said, "I think the March on Washington . . . wasn't a march on Washington. It was a march in Washington. I don't know of any sweeping achievements that came out of it. It was a great ceremony. I would be hard-pressed to identify the substance."[45] But Clarke got ahead of himself with those comments. A year after the march, and certainly influenced by it, Congress passed the Civil Rights Act of 1964, which made segregation in public places illegal, required employers to provide equal employment opportunities, and protected the right of every American to vote, regardless of the color of his skin.[46] This was one of the most important victories of the civil rights movement.

In speaking with Nelson I was so absorbed that I lost track of time, but now our conversation paused and I realized it was getting late. Nelson encouraged me to extend my stay a bit longer, but having absorbed so much history all at once, I knew it was time for me to return home.

The next morning I woke up at three a.m. to get ready for my flight home. By the time I landed in Baltimore, around nine o'clock that morning, I was exhausted. My time in Alabama's hot summer heat and humidity, and hours spent thinking about the blood, sweat, and tears that so many men and women had given to the civil rights movement, so that future generations like mine could have freedom, had wiped me out.

45   *John Henrik Clarke: A Great And Mighty Walk* (1996), Directed by St. Claire Bourne.

46   "The March on Washington for Jobs and Freedom," *PBS Newshour*.

PART II

7: THE AWAKENING

Back in Baltimore, I realized that I had a lot to digest from my second trip to Alabama. That's when I began to wonder exactly when it was that I evolved—when it was that I began to care about civil rights and social justice issues affecting black America. There was a time in my life when I was part of the problems plaguing the African American community—when I was involved in its underground drug economy—but somewhere along the way I changed, and I wanted to become part of the solution.

When I was in Montgomery, listening to Nelson talk about how his father instilled discipline in him and his seven brothers to the extent that none of them ever spent a minute in jail or was ever involved in crime, those remarks got my attention. They made me think about my own life and journey. Growing up in Baltimore, I lived a life that was a lot different than Nelson Malden's. Our story, told through our unusual friendship, is a tale of two lives and two eras, each facing its own unique problems and with its own cast of characters, but with repeating themes of searching for equality and justice.

Much of Baltimore city is rough and rugged, still transitioning from the industrial town it once was to what is now: a mostly low-wage service economy. There were no segregation laws or legal discriminatory policies when I was growing up, but there were still plenty of obstacles for black people, and there continue to be.

Racism in America today is different than it was when Nelson was growing up, or when he was part of the American civil rights movement. Today it's watered down and not as overt as in the past. There aren't cross burnings on the lawns of African American families who move into all-white neighborhoods, but they may end up with unsustainably high interest rates on their mortgages, a problem their white neighbors don't have. There are no segregation era signs designating the use of public water fountains as "Whites Only," but inequities in wealth may force people to live in homes where the water is tainted with high levels of lead and other poisonous chemicals.

In many ways, racism continues to be institutionalized, both socially and economically. The sad truth is that whether it's because of unspoken discrimination or is simply the legacy of four hundred years of oppression from which they have not yet recovered, black Americans are still more likely than white Americans to face routine injustice in their daily lives. I often wonder if a black man is pulled over by a white police officer for speeding, will that officer be more prone to write a ticket than if the driver were a white man? And if a black person commits a criminal offense, will he or she receive the same sentence in a court of law as his white neighbor who committed the same crime? Thinking about whether my black child will be able to close the wealth gap in her lifetime, or whether that burden will be passed along again to the next generation, to her children or grandchildren, keeps me up at night.

Baltimore in the 1970s and 1980s was a totally different environment than Alabama was for Nelson in the 1930s and 1940s, but it was also a totally different time in America. When I was growing up, Bill Cosby was still a role model, long before accusations of Benadryl,

Quaaludes, and sexual abuse. It was just Bill wearing cool sweaters or hoodies with the names of historically black colleges and universities printed on the front. He was the face of the Huxtables, a black upper-middle-class family taking their share of bumps and bruises but still flourishing in America. In those days I was a regular consumer of *The Cosby Show*, and with Bill I laughed at the antics of young Theo and little Rudy.

This depiction of thriving black Americans was a brief breath of fresh air for a kid in Baltimore, where violent crime, drugs, poverty, unemployment, food deserts, chronic homelessness, and health disparities have historically been overwhelming problems for the majority-black population. For decades, these social issues have been a thorn in the side of our political leaders who've struggled to find solutions.

I've seen and experienced a lot of pain in my life, and yet never in a million years did I believe that seeing injustice inflicted upon the underserved, the poor, the widowed, and the marginalized would touch my heart in the way that it has come to. For better or for worse, everyone evolves in life. At some point, we all pivot and change how we see the world. Sometimes those changes are initiated by events that at first seem to have nothing to do with us personally, but then we realize that they have everything to do with us in ways that we never could have imagined.

My personal social justice awakening began with the highly publicized shooting death of seventeen-year-old Trayvon Martin in Sanford, Florida, on February 26, 2012. The twenty-sixth day of February has always been an important day in my life because it's my birthday. On that evening in 2012 when Trayvon Martin was killed, I was out on the town with some friends celebrating. It wasn't a huge gathering, but it was a memorable one. We went to a restaurant where we ordered Maine lobster, Alaskan snow crab legs, filet mignon, and a bunch of other overpriced dishes. By the time we finished eating, we could barely move from the table. From the restaurant, we headed over to a popular lounge and continued the celebration.

Seeing the story on the news a few days later, I thought about what had been happening in Florida while I was celebrating with my friends. That contrast was what first got me interested in a case whose consequences would eventually reverberate across America. It's incredible sometimes how horrendous crimes have a way of grabbing hold of our hearts through the media, leaving us glued to a story. That was exactly what happened to me.

My main thought at that time was what a nightmare it must have been for Trayvon's parents to lose their child in the way that they did. As I continued to view the news coverage of the shooting in the days that followed, I learned exactly where Trayvon's death occurred—in Sanford, Florida. I had been to Sanford many years ago. I'd driven there from Orlando, where I'd stayed for almost a month, taking a much-needed vacation. While bouncing around from place to place in Orlando, I'd realized that I was in desperate need of a haircut; I had been told that the best place to find a barber who could provide me with a good haircut was about forty-five minutes north, in a small town named Sanford. At the time, I didn't think much about the fact that I had to drive forty-five minutes away from a major city just to find a barber who knew how to cut a black person's hair. When I saw the name of the town where young Trayvon lost his life, I was reminded of my brief visit to Sanford, and I was struck by the absurdity of the drive I had to make for a haircut.

Not long after, President Obama mentioned Trayvon's death during a White House press conference. I'll never forget the comment he made on national television: "If I had a son, he would look like Trayvon." After hearing that line from our first African American president, I'm almost certain that every parent in America who has a young black son hugged him even tighter every time he stepped out of their home. It was an awakening identical to that experienced by many Americans after the Bloody Sunday beatings in Selma, or after seeing the photos of Emmett Till following his murder in Mississippi. Average Americans who were once consumed with the details of their own lives began to stand up and participate in an insurgency, a social justice revolution.

When the criminal trial for Trayvon's death began in 2013, the world began to hear more about "stand your ground" laws, the strategy by which Florida and some other states, in my opinion, legalize second-degree murder. As the trial unfolded on live television and George Zimmerman became a household name, the nation began to pay more attention to the case. It was painful to listen to the recorded 911 call from the so-called "community watch volunteer" who fired a bullet from his nine-millimeter handgun into the chest of a seventeen-year-old who had gone to a 7-Eleven convenience store to purchase a bag of Skittles and a bottle of Arizona Ice Tea, like any other teenager might do.

Watching the trial unfold in real time on CNN was riveting, and many Americans felt confident that justice would be served in the case. But by the end of the trial, America's opinion of young black boys wearing hoodies while walking through the dark of night had been revealed once again. And as the verdict was read by the judge, the rest of the world got a chance to feel the sting of injustice that African Americans often experience when we encounter a court of law.

I can only imagine what was going through Trayvon's mind while George Zimmerman was stalking him on that dark night in Florida. Any rational person would have been alarmed by the actions of the irrational wannabe "community watchman." George Zimmerman played the role of a terrorist that night, hoping to evoke fear in a young boy as he walked through the neighborhood, and our criminal justice system let Trayvon down.

While millions of people around the country mourned along with Tracy Martin and Sybrina Fulton, Trayvon's parents, it became clear to me that there was a pattern of unarmed black males being killed in this country. And for the first time that I could remember, it seemed as if some people in the mainstream media were finally saying that the lives of black men in America matter. Over time, those conversations gained even more traction, opening the eyes of others who also began expressing their concern.

Following Trayvon's death in 2012, it seemed as if a rash of extra-judicial killings of unarmed black people by institutional authorities occurred—or maybe we just heard more about them. It was a warm summer day on Thursday, July 17, 2014, on Victory Boulevard and Bay Street in the Tompkinsville area of Staten Island, New York, when Eric Garner was choked to death by a New York City police officer.

Eric Garner was a fixture in the community and known by many, and so was Ramsey Orta,[47] the twenty-four-year-old man who recorded the altercation that day between Garner and members of the New York City Police Department. On the video, Garner can be seen pleading with officers, claiming he wasn't doing anything wrong and accusing police of unfairly harassing him.[48] As the altercation advances in the video, Eric Garner is put in a chokehold by a police officer; you can clearly hear him struggling while saying, "I can't breathe," over and over again—eleven times in all—as the officer continues to apply pressure to his windpipe. America watched the execution of another black man, another supposedly equal citizen, recorded on a cell phone camera.

---

47   Josh Sanburn, "The Witness: One Year After Filming Eric Garner's Fatal Confrontation with Police, Ramsey Orta's Life Has Been Upended," *Time*, July, 2015.

48   Ibid.

In the end, yet again, justice was not served. Though Garner's death was ruled a homicide, the police officer who killed Eric Garner, Daniel Pantaleo, was never indicted and is still employed by the NYPD. And just three weeks after the death of Eric Garner in Staten Island, another tragedy unfolded, this time in Ferguson, Missouri.

A police officer in Ferguson approached eighteen-year-old Michael Brown on August 9, 2014. According to authorities, the officer suspected Brown was involved a convenience store robbery. Officer Darren Wilson fired several shots at the unarmed Brown, six of them striking him, killing him on the scene.[49]

America was watching closely as the news from Ferguson spread, touching off demonstrations and protests in cities around the United States. From San Francisco to Philadelphia, protestors and activists were united by the thousands in letting their voices be heard on the issue of killing unarmed black men in America. Racial tensions were already high in Ferguson, and the shooting of Michael Brown unleashed a fury that had never been seen there before. Within days, Ferguson became the epicenter of rallies and organized demonstrations in America.

For my own part, I had been awakened. I was conscious and focused, and my vision was clear. I wanted to be part of the solution, and so did thousands, if not millions, of other people across the nation.

Social media had become a friend to this new movement, and cell phone video recordings were now a tool of the trade in exposing the truth. I wasn't naïve or green enough to believe that the killing of unarmed black men was new to America. This injustice had been going on for decades and centuries. The big difference now, in this new millennium, was the enhancement of technology and the omnipresence of reliable cell phone cameras. The cell phone camera has become

---

49   Rachael Clarke and Christopher Lett, "What Happened When Michael Brown Met Officer Darren Wilson," CNN, November 11, 2014.

the great equalizer of the world, forcing local, state, and federal law enforcement officials to be more accountable for their actions after evidence of their wrongdoing has been revealed.

The beating of Rodney King, in Los Angeles in 1990, was the first example of how a video recording of excessive force and misconduct by police officers could provide evidence that a crime has been committed by law enforcement officials. More recent events, from the choking of Eric Garner on Staten Island to the arrest in Baltimore of Freddie Gray, who died after losing consciousness in the back of a police van, show how technology has changed the game. Video recordings have lifted the veil, allowing the public to see behind the curtain and get a glimpse of how encounters between black men and police officers have really unfolded for decades. These aren't the watered-down versions of events from the spokespersons for police departments across the United States that the public has been getting for years. These brutal videos of black men being killed are examples of why the relationship between the black community and police officers has been so distressing.

These grotesque recordings that are difficult to watch have ignited fury in a once docile public. Collectively, these events have shocked the conscience of many, forcing millions of people from all walks of life to wake up and to speak out. Overnight, college students, in droves, have turned into activists, and they're motivated to make a difference. America can no longer ignore the injustice that's been beamed into its living rooms via the evening news and that shows up daily on their social media newsfeeds.

There was twelve-year-old Tamir Rice, who was shot and killed by police officers in Cleveland while playing outside of a recreation center with a toy gun. There was Terence Crutcher, shot and killed by a police officer in Tulsa, Oklahoma, in 2016, and Alton Sterling, shot at close range and killed by police officers in Baton Rouge, Louisiana, in 2016. Philando Castile was shot and killed by police officers in a suburb of

St. Paul, Minnesota, in 2016, after informing the officer during a routine traffic stop that he was carrying a licensed handgun, which, by law, he was allowed to do. Philando did everything he should have done during the traffic stop, and yet he was still shot multiple times by the officer. There was also Sandra Bland, who was pulled over for failing to use a turn signal and ended up dead in a Texas jail cell. Sandra Bland was just one of many African Americans who have died unnecessarily in the custody of law enforcement officials.

Sometimes it feels like we're losing count of how many times these tragic incidents have occurred because nowadays they seem more frequent. But this is the way it has always been: What's new is that today there's a camera on just about every corner in America, and what was once unseen is now frequently viewed by us all. While American communities have become traumatized by these videos, our politicians, who have the power to make the needed changes in laws and policies, have seemingly become even more desensitized to them.

I wonder sometimes how many more killings of unarmed black men committed by police officers would have been prosecuted if there had been videos of those incidents. What if there had been amateur videographers recording with their cellphones throughout the 1990s? What would we have seen? Even with video evidence, very few police officers have been charged with crimes in these incidents, and even fewer convicted. And yet, imagine if Ramsey Orta had not been on Staten Island that day, recording as Daniel Pantaleo was choking Eric Garner. What if Kevin Moore had not been there making a recording of the arrest of Freddie Gray in Baltimore, which ultimately became a crucial piece of evidence against the six police officers who were charged in the case? What if Philando Castile's girlfriend, Diamond Reynolds, hadn't been there that fateful day to post his killing by a police officer on Facebook Live for the world to see?

In 2015, a brave bystander in Charleston, South Carolina, recorded the execution of Walter Scott by a white police officer who opened fire on him as he ran away, shooting the unarmed Scott in the back. How would that case have unfolded if Feidin Santana had not been there that day with his cell phone camera, recording as Officer Michael Slager staged the crime scene to cover up the shooting? Slager was sentenced to twenty years in prison for murder, in addition to a federal conviction on civil rights charges. If not for the video, the resolution of that case would have been partially reliant on a crooked cop's word regarding what happened, pitted against that of a dead man who couldn't speak for himself.

With this ugly history in America, how can a person not understand the skepticism of black people and activists, when unarmed black men are killed by police officers? Because of this long history of brutalization, the credibility of law enforcement officials is not unimpeachable, and it deserves to be scrutinized by the public.

That's why I've become an advocate for the mass implementation of body cameras for officers in police departments throughout this country: I believe they can make a difference. I think that body cameras worn by officers will force the ones who don't do their jobs correctly to improve—but this outcome is still predicated on officers having the proper training. Training can mean the difference between an officer being able to successfully apply community policing strategies, like getting to know residents and working with them to identify and solve problems, and a riot and uprising in the streets following the unjustified shooting of another unarmed African American.

As citizens, we were wrong to blindly trust our criminal justice system for centuries and hand over a blank check to our police departments without demanding the maximum amount of accountability. We must scrutinize our system at every turn to ensure that every single person confronted, arrested, or detained receives all that the US Constitution guarantees them.

Think about the response in Baltimore in 2015 when twenty-five-year-old Freddie Gray, while in the custody of the Baltimore police, was arrested and critically injured, and later died. Today, many people are still wondering how the bungled arrest of one man could have led to an uprising that paralyzed a major American city. Underneath that question lies yet another question: Why did the police officers make the decision to pursue Freddie Gray in the first place? The police initially stopped Gray because he "fled unprovoked upon noticing police presence," according to charging documents written by Officer Garrett Miller and cited by the *Baltimore Sun*.[50]

But many law enforcement professionals had questions about that arrest: "Did [police] have a right to stop him in the first place?" asked Chuck Drago, a former police chief in Florida.[51] Central to that question is the issue of "zero-tolerance" or "broken windows" policing, which basically involves cracking down on minor offenses in the hope of reducing major crime as well.[52] The problem with that strategy is that by arresting so many people for petty crimes, by the time you get to the "big fish," you've antagonized an entire community, straining relationships there beyond tolerance. Journalist Eugene Robinson made an important point when he wrote, "If police concentrate their patrols in a certain area and assume every young man they see is a potential or probable criminal, they will conduct more searches—and make more arrests."[53] According to reports, Freddie Gray had been arrested eighteen times over an eight-year period. All the arrests were for nonviolent offenses, except one arrest for assault.

50   Christina Sterbenz, "A 'Big Question' Surrounds the Arrest of Freddie Gray, Which Sparked Riots Across Baltimore," *Business Insider*, April 30, 2015.

51   Ibid.

52   Eugene Robinson, "It's Time to Seriously Rethink 'Zero Tolerance' Policing," *Washington Post*, May 4, 2015.

53   Ibid.

The death of Freddie Gray was the call to action, but there were decades of built-up frustration behind it. Long before Freddie Gray was arrested in his Sandtown-Winchester neighborhood and the rebellion in the streets began, that same part of town—where decades earlier legendary jazz icons Billie Holiday, Eubie Blake, and Scott Joplin roamed the streets—harbored a dirty little secret. Poor living conditions had been a way of life there since before the 1968 riots in Baltimore that followed the assassination of Dr. Martin Luther King Jr., and they have never been resolved. Poverty and decay decimated the once bustling black community and has remained high for a long time. It has been reported that in Freddie Gray's old neighborhood, more than a third of households are in poverty.[54] These numbers would be unacceptable in almost any other municipality in the United States, but they have been Baltimore's dark, ugly secret for some time now. It's not hard to confirm the pain that exists. When Freddie Gray was shot, 51.2 percent of the households in his neighborhood had an income of less than $25,000.[55] Senator Bernie Sanders toured Gray's West Baltimore neighborhood and likened it to a Third World country.[56]

So while the spark that ignited the unrest in Baltimore was the video of the officers loading Freddie Gray into the back of a police vehicle, the fuel had been lying in the streets for years, camouflaged under poverty, unemployment, trauma, a broken education system, and hopelessness. Freddie Gray became a symbol of a community that had become exhausted by mistreatment.

When the police department is focused on arresting people for minor, nonviolent infractions, valuable resources are wasted. When African American men compile long criminal records consisting of

---

54 Jana Kasperkevic, "In Freddie Gray's Neighborhood, More than a Third of Households are in Poverty," *The Guardian*," April 28, 2015.

55 Ibid.

56 John Fritze, "Bernie Sanders likens West Baltimore to 'Third World' country," *The Baltimore Sun*, December 8, 2015.

low-level offenses like loitering, littering, and simple possession of drugs, everyone loses, especially the community. One of the most pragmatic comments I've read regarding this subject was made by the *Washington Post*'s Eugene Robinson, who wrote: "The first two steps toward uplifting young black men are simple: Stop killing them and stop locking them in prison for nonviolent offenses."[57]

———

So, what now? What kind of racial reconciliation is possible when we have racists walking the streets of America with no fear of retribution, carrying tiki torches and chanting their hatred in vernacular that was crafted one hundred years ago? In an article entitled "Where Do We Go from Here? Racial Reconciliation in 2017," Matthew J. Hall asks this question for the Ethics and Religious Liberty Commission of the Southern Baptist Convention. He cites the question that Martin Luther King Jr. faced in 1967, a time when "violence, hatred and anger had engulfed much of the country." Back then, King called for nonviolent demonstrations as a form of direct action and protest.[58] He also spoke of the "fierce urgency of now" in his famous speech at the March on Washington. In his view, this call to direct action was rooted in a "biblical vision of the world and God's purposes."

Looking around at the racial violence being perpetrated in America today, some concerned citizens might wonder whether there is realistic hope for an implementation of King's nonviolent demonstration approach. How can such indifference to human dignity be met with nonviolent force? As Hall emphasizes, King also spoke about love being the highest good. While simple optimism, a belief that others

57   Robinson, "It's Time to Seriously Rethink 'Zero Tolerance' Policing."

58   Mathew J. Hall, "Where Do We Go From Here? Racial Reconciliation in 2017," Ethics and Religious Liberty Commission of the Southern Baptist Convention, 2017.

will easily change their minds and see the light, may no longer be enough to inspire us, a more enduring attitude is that in spite of the challenges, we can continue to focus on hope and love—"love for God, love for neighbor."

The ideal should be to replace hate and anger with love, but we also need to reform the social and legal systems that continue to undermine racial equality in this country. One important aspect of the marches in Selma that people watching them on television may have not understood was that the protests started not with an abstract idea, but with very practical concerns: voter registration and the right to vote without discrimination. Voter registration is important because voting is not only critical for full participation in a democracy and electing the candidates you support, but it also directly affects the court system and the justice system; the connection between the two was critical for black people in Selma.

Registering to vote is also the only way for your name to get into a jury pool. The jury pools for the county courts are compiled from the county's list of registered voters. If African Americans couldn't register to vote, that also meant that their names wouldn't be part of the pools to be called to serve on a jury. So, the phrase "a jury of your peers" was rarely applicable to a black defendant in a Selma courtroom, who most often would be left facing an all-white jury. As a result, there were massive disparities in conviction and sentencing outcomes for black defendants, compared to white defendants charged with the same crime.

Nelson once told me that "It's important to have discussions today about the lynchings that occurred in the South and how unconscionable they were, but rarely do we talk about the thousands of 'courtroom lynchings' that took place then." If you were unlucky enough to find yourself in a courtroom facing a jury trial, and two or three of the jury members were also Klan members, you were probably in big trouble.

There are black people still serving time in penitentiaries today because of the injustice done to them in the court system, not only in Selma, but all around the United States. The court system wasn't kind or even fair to blacks back then, and it still isn't today.

8: I AM A BLACK MAN

As young kid, I hated watching the award-winning television miniseries *Roots*, which is considered a classic today. Everything about it hurt me to my core. I detested how black people were depicted on the prime-time show, I despised how they were treated by the slave owners, and most of all, I hated how watching it made me feel.

At the time, *Roots* was one of the biggest programs to ever land on a television screen in America, attracting more than 130 million[59] viewers at a time when the population of the United States was only around 220 million people. That's an astonishing number of viewers for a television drama that sought to teach and enlighten its viewers about a brutal time in our history.

When I was a kid, my family owned one black-and-white television set that we had to share—all six of us. Do you remember having the kind of television that required you to wrap aluminum foil around the antenna just to get enough reception to watch the same three lousy TV stations? On top of this, our TV was so old that eventually we had to change the channel using a set of pliers after the knob broke off. It was just another day in the hood. Sad excuse for a TV though it was, all six members of my household had to negotiate time to watch

---

59   Frank Rich, "Television: A Super Sequel to Haley's Comet," *Time*, February 18, 1979.

this monstrosity, and that often became a problem. There were many days when physical fights broke out right there in the middle of the living room over whether to watch *Scooby-Doo*, *The Cosby Show*, or Oprah Winfrey.

So when it came time to watch those highly acclaimed, popular television shows like *Roots*, I didn't have much of a choice. My vote was overruled by my mother and father, who insisted that we all watch *Roots* together and become "enlightened" by an important black American story. But it was terrifying for me to see those bloody wounds on the naked backs of slaves who had been savagely beaten by white human traffickers. Even today, I've still never watched the show in its entirety. I still can't. It makes me cringe and it makes me angry. I might be the only black person in America today who grew up in the 1980s and hasn't seen all of Alex Haley's epic work.

Seeing black men and women in shackles, with rusty chains wrapped around their necks, being tormented and treated like wild animals, made me nauseous, ashamed of being black, and depressed about being a young and poor person of color. It brought out a self-hatred in me that was already alive and thriving, to the degree that I thought something must be wrong with me. I was embarrassed and afraid of having brown skin; if having brown skin meant that I might have to endure the kind of savagery that I saw on *Roots*, I didn't want to be black.

Today, I understand why the series affected me the way that it did. It was a representation of white supremacy at a time when I, a young child, didn't even understand what "white supremacy" meant. I was far too young to comprehend it, but I knew something wasn't right about those merciless scenes on the screen. All I knew was that Kunta Kinte shouldn't have been beaten that way. I knew that the wounds from that white man's whip shouldn't have been there on that black boy's back, and that the brutal amputation of Toby's right foot as punishment for running away from his white owner should never have happened. Even as a young kid, I knew something was terribly wrong with that picture, and I didn't want to have anything to do with it. I didn't feel great and uplifted after seeing the stereotypes shown on screen and the degradation of people of color. I wasn't inspired.

And yet, *Roots* was the talk of America among scholars, educators, and the common man. Even at my small elementary school in West Baltimore, everyone was talking about it. Many of the white school-teachers at Rognel Heights Elementary School could be overheard saying that watching the series the previous night had "changed their lives." They talked about how enlightened they had become about the plight of black people in America—as if it hadn't been there for them to see all along. It was white savior complex at its finest.

And, of course, the other young students in my classroom had opinions they wanted to express about the show. School-aged children can be cruel and callous, and in this case, they were on their worst behavior. Many of the students in my class who watched the show would return to school the next day mocking the character Kunta Kinte. They talked in negative terms about the way he looked, his "nappy" hair and his "black dark skin." These were black students who made disparaging comments about the way Kunta Kinte talked and the way he cried. Their oppression had been turned inward. He was black, appalling, and in their eyes, a terrible human being for becoming a "stupid" slave. After watching *Roots*, I hated my blackness. It took years for me to get rid of the self-hatred I had developed.

Black boys are often damaged in ways that most people would never understand by seeing negative images and stereotypes of themselves in the media. Not only do they constantly see black faces that look like them being dehumanized in the media, they also see black men and boys in every aspect of their daily lives being dehumanized and objectified. The coarseness of their hair and the darkness of their skin are often met with insult in overt and subliminal ways. Being stopped and frisked, being followed by staff in stores, being treated harshly when they're being rambunctious, in a way that teenagers of other races would get away with.

Fortunately for me, years later, those negative thoughts and feelings about myself began to gradually dissipate and I began to love who I was and love my black culture. My conversion began around the same time that I fell in love . . . with hip-hop. It all started for me when I first heard the rap group Public Enemy and Chuck D, speaking to the world as forcefully as they could: "Here is a land that never gave a damn / about a brother like me and myself because they never did."[60] It was the lyrics of hip-hop music that spoke about the realities of black America, rapped and sung by people of color, like me, that fixed me when I was broken. When old school rappers like Eric B. and Rakim said, "I'm just an addict, addicted to music / maybe it's a habit . . . I gotta use it,"[61] I was healed. Those words spoke to me in powerful terms, as did seeing the visuals of strong black men and women speaking truth to power with no fear, and rejecting any notion that the blackness of African American men and women wasn't bold and beautiful. Hip-hop culture was a lifeline for me when I was in my late teens; it breathed spirit into an empty vessel that desperately sought inspiration and something to hold onto.

Just a few years later, the rapper Ice Cube, part of the hip-hop group N.W.A., said, "Fuck tha police,"[62] upsetting the white establishment, which already viewed hip-hop as dangerous. But then Queen Latifah got on the stage and spoke about positivity while celebrating

---

60 "Black Steel in the Hour of Chaos" (Artist: Public Enemy), 1988.

61 "I Ain't No Joke" (Artists: Eric B. & Rakim and Louis Eric Barrier), 1987.

62 "Fuck Tha Police" (Artist: N.W.A.), 1988.

life in her lyrics: "Well it's a beautiful day in the neighborhood, a beautiful day in the neighborhood / can't go wrong, I feel strong and the flavor's good."[63]

The harmony of the masterful music combined with lyrical mosaics of black power ignited my inner flame, even while it drew the ire of some in corporate America and on Capitol Hill. While America wanted us to be straitlaced, taking inspiration from the character Carlton Banks on *The Fresh Prince of Bel-Air*, many of us wanted to be rebels like Tupac Shakur. Hip-hop and rap music spoke unapologetically to the experiences of young black youth who weren't sure how to articulate their struggle in America. It was the "rebirth of a nation," as Public Enemy called it, and suddenly we all wanted to be like Nat Turner, the black revolutionary, and not like O. J. Simpson. It was hip-hop that brought my blackness alive.

Black music, like hip-hop and rap, which was born in the basement of a Bronx tenement, gave millions of young people of color a platform to love who they were. We didn't just fall in love with the music, we fell in love with the culture. Hip-hop made it cool to be black and proud, and then, suddenly, blackness was in vogue. Suddenly everyone from Brooklyn to Los Angeles wanted a piece of the culture. From Jewish kids living in New Jersey, attending services at the synagogue, to the wealthy white kids living in Hollywood Hills mansions, everyone wanted to wear Adidas sweat suits and sport fresh sneakers with fat shoelaces. Black culture was in style. And the message that black is beautiful wasn't just hyperbole, it was something deeper.

Even after Tupac Shakur's character in the movie *Juice* was pushed off the rooftop and died on the cold concrete, hip-hop survived the fall. After two decades of hip-hop growth, music industry culture vultures finally came out of the shadows to rob and steal every piece

---

63   "Just Another Day" (Artist: Queen Latifah), 1993.

of black content that wasn't nailed down or copyrighted. Suddenly corporate America saw value in our blackness and wanted a piece of the pie for their Walmart jingles and Old Navy commercials airing in white suburbia.

Even today, hip-hop music and black culture continue to evolve. Kendrick Lamar, Common, Jay-Z, and Beyoncé are here to remind us all that blackness and the "culture" are worthy of notice and can be enjoyed by people of all races, and also that every day we are rewriting the black American story.

I remember those early days of hip-hop well, as well as the feeling of not being sure who I was or what I was. Over time I evolved and grew as a person and as a black man, but today I'm concerned about the young brothers who may be struggling to find their identity in this America. I often wonder how many of them are truly proud when they look in the mirror, how many of them can shout to themselves, "I am a black man!"

———

In January 2017, I boarded a flight from Baltimore to Houston, Texas, for a speaking engagement at Texas Southern University. I had been invited to speak to one hundred college students, many of whom would soon be leaders out in the world. When I arrived in the Lone Star State, I was excited about the upcoming presentation. It warms my heart whenever I can talk to students attending historically black colleges and universities (HBCUs). Before visiting Texas Southern, I had presented at more than two dozen other colleges and universities around the United States, the bulk of them HBCUs.

I arrived two days before my scheduled appearance so I could get some rest and prepare for the upcoming engagement. At that point, I had been traveling a lot, and I needed to breathe easy for a moment.

On one of my free days, I took a short tour around the "Magnolia City," expecting to see hundreds of white men in cowboy hats and boots—talk about a stereotype. To my surprise, I saw a lot of black people walking around the city.

In my presentation I spoke about "making positive life choices" and social issues affecting black communities; afterward I felt energized. The minds of college students are like blank canvasses just waiting to become colorful masterpieces. I enjoy every minute I get to interact with students at HBCUs, because I see them as our future: the doctors, teachers, politicians, and social workers who will lead us one day. They motivate me just as much as I hope I motivate them, because I can see firsthand how focused they are on creating a life for themselves. These are the black boys and girls who are doing everything they're supposed to be doing, who will never make headlines on the evening news, because their lives aren't negative enough. Their stories aren't the stories that most news producers and reporters want to air on prime-time television. They've made their pursuit of education a top priority because they understand its value. They're going about their daily lives focused on the future, using education as the tool to build that future.

It was there at Texas Southern University that I started to have an epiphany about my legacy as a black man. I began to think about the contribution I've made to society. What have I done for the world? Meeting Nelson and learning about the civil rights movement had sparked something in me. It had forced me to think about my own contribution and the things I have or have not done to make a difference.

At the same time, I began to think more about the issue of education. Acquiring a quality education is the only way that African Americans will break the cycle of generational poverty that continues to plague our communities. Poverty is the real Achilles' heel of black America. Nelson had talked to me about the wrath of poverty in the

South before and after the civil rights movement, and his words reiterated to me why it is so important for a black person to make education a priority in life.

An education is the only way out of poverty, especially generational poverty. It's the key to a livable wage, which can give a person the ability to build a decent life for themselves and their family. And if a person really wants to be considered an educated person who is knowledgeable about the world, that person must also be knowledgeable about who he or she is. I'm not referring to being knowledgeable about the kind of things they ask you on a Match.com questionnaire when looking for a date. I'm referring to the deep, intricate details that you think about in the middle of the night when you're in bed alone: Who am I? What am I? What makes me tick? What are my strengths? What are my weaknesses? How was life for my ancestors? A person must know these things if they want to truly understand who they are. You can't understand the world when you don't understand yourself.

One day when I was talking with Nelson, I was struck by the realization that I didn't know much about who I am. We were sitting in his living room and he was telling me about his family background, including details about his grandfather who was a slave and about his grandmother who was mixed race. He also told me a bit about the generation before them. Nelson knew more about the heritage of his family than almost any black person I have ever spoken with about that issue, and much more than I did. The knowledge I had of my family history ended with my paternal grandmother and grandfather. I knew next to nothing about the generation prior to them. I certainly couldn't share stories about where they came from, what they were like as people, or what they did for work. I wondered if finding out about my family heritage could help me answer questions about myself.

Most African Americans have minimal knowledge of their family's heritage. Some have no knowledge at all about the blood relatives who came before them, and many of us have no way of tracing our family's lineage back to the country of our ancestral origin. When African slaves arrived in the Americas and were purchased by white slave owners, the slaves weren't given a last name. Because of this, it's difficult to trace an African American's family heritage prior to our ancestors' arrival in the United States.

Leaving the TSU campus after my talk, I returned to my hotel. As I sat there on the edge of my bed, a commercial appeared on the television in my room that piqued my interest. The commercial was from a company that helps customers track their lineages with DNA tests. I became intrigued as they explained how they search the world's largest online family history resources so users can discover who their ancestors were and learn more about their ethnicity. After seeing that commercial, a light bulb went on in my head. In my presentation to the students at Texas Southern, I had asked them a few rhetorical questions that I hoped would spark some discussion.

"Who are you? What are you?"

As I sat there on the bed, I realized that taking a DNA test could answer some of those questions for me, the same ones that had come up when Nelson told me about his family lineage. The test could help me discover information about my own family's lineage and ultimately about myself. So, I grabbed my laptop and went online to purchase a test kit. Just a few days later, a medium-sized package arrived at my home. It all happened a lot faster than I had anticipated. I was excited and a bit nervous, but I immediately opened the package. I was anticipating that something important was going to happen. Following the directions, I spit into a small plastic container, sealed it shut, and placed the container inside a plastic bag that I then deposited into the prepaid envelope and mailed back to the company. It was that easy, and for the next few weeks I didn't think much more about it.

About six weeks later, I received an email notifying me that my

DNA test results were ready for my review. It was like a huge window into the past that had once been nailed shut was about to open. I was excited, but I also wanted to be able to take it all in. I took a moment to calm and center myself and then I clicked on the link in the email and began to review the results. I was initially overwhelmed by the amount of detail they provided. It was astonishing, as if the sea had parted and I could see directly across the Atlantic and back into time. I could envision my ancestors there, in their place of birth, sitting around an open fire hundreds of years ago.

I began my review of the report by reading the section titled "Ethnicity Estimate." According to the company, the Ethnicity Estimate shows where your ancestors came from, hundreds of thousands of years ago. They calculate it by comparing your DNA to the DNA of a reference panel of others with deep roots in specific places around the world.

The first line I read wasn't much of a surprise: it stated that my Ethnicity Estimate indicated that 79 percent of my DNA traces back to the continent of Africa. Of that number, 29 percent traces specifically to the country of Nigeria. I hadn't expected to see that, but then I thought about a comment a good friend often made to me. She would tell me that I have high cheekbones. A couple times she said, "You must be Nigerian or something." I thought, *Who pays attention to cheekbones?*

The remaining Ethnicity Estimate results from Africa indicated that 13 percent of my DNA can be traced back to a region which is now the countries of Ivory Coast and Ghana, 12 percent from a region which is now the countries of Benin and Togo, another 12 percent from Senegal, 6 percent from a group of people known as the "Africa Southeastern Bantu," 4 percent from Mali, and 2 percent from Cameroon and Congo. Finally, 1 percent of my DNA could be traced to a group described as "African South-Central Hunter-Gatherers."

The other results from my Ethnicity Estimate indicated that 19 percent of my DNA was European. Now that was a huge surprise—not that I possessed European DNA, but how high the amount seemed to be. The breakdown of my European DNA was 7 percent from Scandinavia, 4 percent from Great Britain, 3 percent from Ireland, 2 percent from "Europe West" and 1 percent from Italy/Greece. All the other markers indicated just trace amounts of DNA from "West Asia" and "Europe East."

The most shocking result was that my test indicated that I possessed 0 percent Native American DNA. This was a real surprise! I had been certain that my great-grandmother was part Native American—Cherokee, to be exact—and I repeated that assertion to anyone who would listen, including Nelson. A Native American ancestor was one of the many things, I thought, that we had in common. My family had told me this "fact" many years ago, when I was a young child. It was a story that had circulated through my family for decades. Throughout my lifetime, I've probably told thousands of people that my great-grandmother was part Cherokee—*thousands*! Immediately, I imagined myself being on the Maury Povich Show following a DNA test and being informed by the host of the show that "Kevin, you are *not* the father."

After getting the news, I called my sister on the phone.

"Hey, I must have been the baby who got mixed up at the hospital, because it turns out I don't have any Native American DNA."

She was baffled at first, "How's that possible? You know that great-grandma was half Cherokee!"

My older sister, who enjoyed the mystique of having Native American ancestors, was in denial, and I could see why. We'd always had this visual in our minds of our great-grandmother sitting on a reservation in South Carolina, wearing a natural feather headdress and moccasins and cooking over an open fire. But now that tale had been seriously debunked.

My sister and I laughed about it, but then I was reminded of a conversation I'd had with a friend a few months earlier. I was telling him about my family having Cherokee lineage, and he began to caution me. He basically warned me that it's a common myth that many black families think they have Native American ancestors and that most really have none. I didn't think much of it at the time. Now, I felt a little silly for having been so certain that I did.

The DNA test results also had a section titled "Genetic Communities" that shows where your family probably lived in the past few hundred years. According to the test company, they create this information by identifying groups of people who have taken the DNA test who are genetically connected to one another. My results placed my family in three location groups here in the United States: African Americans on the South Carolina–North Carolina border, African Americans in the Mid-Atlantic states, and African Americans in northern and central Virginia. This information made me think that maybe I'd once, as a kid, heard about family members living in some of those areas. But I couldn't remember for sure and even if that was the case, it was hearsay. I didn't have any names and there was no one to ask. After my grandfather died of lung cancer when I was young, most of the members of my family seemed to just go their own separate ways. The glue of a positive black male role model was no longer there to keep the family together.

Just thinking about my African heritage was a lot to take in. I had no understanding of what it was like to stand on the continent, surrounded by its many cultures. I had no idea what it meant to be an African native. We have all kinds of stereotypes and misinformation about Africa, and limited substantive facts. I didn't even know, until about a decade ago, that the continent of Africa was comprised of fifty-three separate and distinct nations. I guess I missed that in social studies class.

When I speak with people of other races about their family history and they're knowledgeable about their genealogy, I can't help but feel envious. When I talk with whites, Asians, and Hispanics, many of them speak proudly about their long lineage. But for most African Americans, there's a point beyond which it's almost impossible to trace one's lineage because no written records exist. For the young black boy or girl who wants to learn and understand more about his or her heritage, it can be a daunting task. It's almost like looking into a black hole in outer space, having no idea if anything exists there. That can leave any person feeling empty inside, hollow and incomplete. Part of your identity, who you are, originated in the past, many generations before you.

Having the DNA results answered a lot of questions for me, but they also made me hungrier for more information. I needed more substance. I needed to add faces and names to the equation. Who were these people, my ancestors, who left this trail of DNA evidence?

I could conduct various searches on the DNA testing company's database, which allowed me to dive deeper into the archives of the past. That was where I found a 1940 United States Federal Census Report that contained information about my paternal grandfather and grandmother, adding pieces to the puzzle. According to the census document, my paternal grandparents arrived in Baltimore, Maryland, from South Carolina around 1938. When I first saw the document online, my imagination began running wild. I began to imagine my grandparents, then only in their early twenties, journeying to the North on an old train en route to Baltimore. They could have been taking the same route that freed slaves used almost a century before to escape the treacherous South. I couldn't help but wonder what that experience was like.

According to this report, my grandparents came to Baltimore with my grandmother's thirty-six-year-old brother, Edward Washington. The document indicated that my grandfather's occupation was steel worker, and that he worked forty-four hours per week, earning an annual salary of $1,200 in 1939. The 1940 census also indicated that my grandparents had a one-year-old son at the time, my uncle Sonny, and an infant son, my uncle William. But there was a piece of information in the report that I found bothersome: My grandfather's highest grade completed in school was eighth grade, and my grandmother's highest grade completed was seventh grade. Maybe that was just a sign of what those years were like, but I couldn't help wonder how having such a minimal education may have affected their lives.

My grandmother Wilhelmina Shird was from a small town in South Carolina named Camden, and my grandfather Gradie Shird was from an even smaller town named Hodges. The town of Hodges had a population of one hundred and fifty-eight residents. Seeing that information online made me smile, because today there are probably more people than that living on my street. By contrast, Camden was much bigger that Hodges. Camden is now a city inside the metropolitan area of Columbia, South Carolina, though it was presumably smaller in the days when my grandmother grew up there. What wasn't in the report was why my grandparents left South Carolina and came to Baltimore in the first place. Were they running away from something? Did they just wake up one morning and say, "Hey, let's leave our lives behind here in South Carolina and move north?"

The document made me think that since I couldn't learn more about my family history through word of mouth, maybe there was a paper trail. A friend of mine suggested that I contact the Reginald F. Lewis Museum in Baltimore, which houses a research center that conducts genealogy research, so I scheduled an appointment to meet with a genealogist there. The specialist with whom I was assigned to work that day, Lisa, was extremely knowledgeable about genealogy research and African American history.

"Mr. Shird, before you leave today, I'm going to make sure that you know a lot more about your family than you did when you got here. To begin, do you know the state where any of your grandparents were born?" For the first time, I had an answer to this question. It felt good to share one.

We began the search looking for a paper trail that could lead us to my grandfather Gradie, but that didn't work out so well. We searched the computer database for about thirty minutes, and other than the 1940 United States Federal Census Report I had found on my own, we couldn't find anything else related to him—not one single trace.

"Don't let that discourage you, because that often happens. Let's look up your grandmother and see if she's in the database. What was her maiden name?"

"Washington."

We began searching for information on my grandmother and found a match on an often-used database named "Family Search." A wealth of data appeared on the computer screen after just a few clicks of the mouse.

"That's her right there," Lisa said. "And that's probably her mother and her siblings."

In a United States Federal Census Report from 1920, we located information on my grandmother, my great-grandmother, and other members of our family who appeared to be her brothers and sisters. Just looking at the image of the aged document on a computer screen full of handwritten forms from almost one hundred years ago was incredible. It was like walking into a dark tunnel and emerging with a treasure even more valuable than the one you were seeking. According to the document, my great-grandmother Mary Washington was born in March 1883 in Kershaw County, South Carolina. Mary had a third-grade education, her occupation was listed as "laborer on a farm," and by the year 1920, she had six children.

Using the information that we located about my great-grandmother Mary, we started fishing again. This time, the genealogy specialist began her database search using a census report from the year 1900. Through that search, we located information about the mother of my great-grandmother. The genealogist referred to her as my second great-grandmother. Her name was Hana Washington, and she was born around 1862 in the state of Mississippi. She was the mother of nine children, with one of them being my great-grandmother. It was mind-boggling to me that we could find the information, and even Lisa was excited.

"Kevin, you hit pay dirt today. It's rare that we can go back this far in our searches and find information."

As I continued to read the documents, I spotted a bombshell. While reading the demographics listed on the census report for my great-grandmother Mary Washington, I glanced at the "race" category. Her race was listed as "mulatto," which is one of those crude, outdated terms used to describe a mixed-race person. She had a black and a white parent. The census report that contained information about my second great-grandmother indicated that she was black, so the father of my great-grandmother had to be a white man. The pieces of the puzzle were coming together in ways that I had not expected, and again the "Cherokee blood line" myth that had been interjected into my family tree decades ago had been debunked. My great-grandmother's race was a mix of black and white, so this old tale that had been around for generations that she was half Native American was definitely false. It was like we had opened a Pandora's box that had been closed for a century.

But now I had questions that I didn't think I would ever find the answers to: Did my grandmother know that this story wasn't true? Was this a deep, dark family secret that had been concealed for a century? Hana Washington, my great great-grandmother, had to know that the father of her daughter, Mary Washington, was a white man, didn't she? Why would Mary Washington list her race in the 1920 United States Census Report as mulatto if that wasn't the case? How many years ago did this untruth begin? Did my grandmother Wilhelmina know that her mother was mixed, with European ancestry and not Native American? Had my grandmother ever been told the truth, or did she die never knowing?

I've heard about black people claiming Native American ancestry to evade the discussion of consensual or unwanted sexual interactions with white people because of fear of retribution. Were my grandparents running away from South Carolina to escape the possibility of a family secret being exposed? I was baffled and throwing different scenarios in the wind to see if they stuck, but the truth was, I had no idea. There was one thing that was clear: The environment in the South in those years was a toxic place for blacks. The way that white Southerners approached the issue of race was oppressive and often barbaric. Being of mixed race in South Carolina in those years was problematic on many levels. Even mixed-race marriages were illegal in many states in the South at the time my grandparents lived there. The state of South Carolina added a ban on interracial marriages to the state constitution in 1895.[64] That ban wasn't removed from the state constitution until 1998, which is incredible when you think about it: Until about two decades ago, interracial marriages in South Carolina were technically illegal and could have sent two individuals of different races, who simply fell in love and wanted a wedding to celebrate

---

64   Sue Anne Pressley, "South Carolina's Racial Relic," *Washington Post*, November 3, 1998.

it, to *jail*. I was blown away to see that this draconian law was still on the books in the 1990s.

And if interracial marriages were punishable by a term of imprisonment, then imagine the level of stigma that existed in the South regarding the children resulting from an interracial relationship, like my great-grandmother. Life for mixed-race children forced to navigate the racist Jim Crow South had to be extremely difficult.

As I learned more about South Carolina, what I found only reinforced the hypothesis I had begun to form: That my grandparents may at some point simply have said to themselves, "Let's get the hell out of here and move north." They may not have just casually left the South in search of better opportunities—they may have been running as fast as they could to get to safety.

That was certainly true of many people of color during the "Great Migration" in the United States, between 1916 and 1970, during which time more than six million African Americans[65] moved from Southern states to live in Northern states. For many it was a matter of life or death—they were running not just toward a better life, but also away from fear.

My head was spinning with all this new information, and I was trying to process everything. The technology we have today that can help us look deep into the past is incredible. Sometimes I wonder if I had known more about my lineage when I was a young man trying to understand the world, would I have made different decisions about my life? Would I have felt differently about my blackness? Would knowing my heritage have given me a greater sense of value, self-esteem, and respect for my life? Would I have had a better understanding of my responsibility to make positive life choices, to protect the Shird name? Seeing the names and details of my forebears, born as much as 150 years ago, affected me in ways that were hard to explain.

---

65   James Ryerson, "Race in America After the Great Migration," *New York Times*, November 18, 2016.

I believe that most people would love to know more about the origin of their families. I'm sure that many young people have thought, from time to time, about learning who they are by learning more about their ancestors. I get it now. It's vital for every person to know his or her roots, because knowing that information can add value to your life.

When I called Nelson on the phone to tell him what I had discovered through the DNA test, like the confirmation that my great-grandmother wasn't part Native American after all, he wasn't impressed. "You didn't have to spend all that time and money just to find that out," he said. "I could have told you that you didn't have no Cherokee Indian in your blood. Black people have been telling those lies for over one hundred years."

All I could do at that point was laugh!

9: DON'T BOO, VOTE

During President Barack Obama's campaign rallies in 2008 and 2012, while he was running for the presidency, his enthusiastic audiences would boo when he mentioned his opponents and their conservative political views: "Don't boo, *vote*," he would say. Obama understood the importance of voting. He needed his supporters to vote so that he could win the presidency, but he also wanted people to exercise their right to do so. This was a right that black people fought hard to attain and he knew this. Seeing a black man become president who understood what other black people had gone through to gain their voting rights meant so much to Nelson.

Just think for a minute about the time when Obama was running for president and he went to Germany, where he was greeted by 250,000 Germans waving the American flag. That was a powerful moment, but then think about how decades earlier in Germany, when a black world-class track athlete named Jesse Owens won the gold medal in the Olympics, Adolph Hitler turned his back on him during the awards ceremony. Not only did Hitler hate Jewish people, he also hated blacks.

Obama winning the election is an issue close to my and my wife's hearts. It was a surreal time for us in 2008 when he won that first election. I mean, Election Night had a very strange and weird feel to it. We were watching the poll results on television and couldn't believe that he won. We couldn't believe that a black man had finally become the president of the United States, after all that we had gone through. Tears were slowly rolling down my face for the remainder of the night. It was unbelievable.

But Nelson's reaction wasn't entirely positive.

The entire time that he was the president, I think that all of us who were around during the civil rights movement were fearful that something would happen to him while he was in office. For the entire eight years that he was there, that thought never left our minds. We were afraid for him as well as his family, and we weren't certain if he would make it out of there.

Nelson explained that it wasn't just the terrible memories of Martin Luther King Jr. being assassinated that had him concerned for our first black president. During the civil rights movement, there were a string of political and organizational leaders who were killed for their advocacy for the rights of people of color, among them: Medgar Evers of the Mississippi NAACP, Harry and Harriette Moore, Malcolm X, John F. Kennedy, Robert Kennedy, and the three young civil rights activists who were killed in 1964 in Mississippi, James Chaney, Andrew Goodman, and Mickey Schwerner. The threat of violence was a tool used by the anti-civil rights segregationists to shut people down when they were too loud or when then gained too much power.

When Nelson said that he was worried about President Obama and the safety of the first black family in the White House because of the history of losing leaders, especially black leaders, I think that he was voicing an opinion that many people across America shared, even if they were afraid to say so and didn't want to give voice to the fear. I can unequivocally say that I wasn't sure if President Obama could weather the cascade of vitriol and hatred directed at him from so many people who couldn't handle the fact that a black man was the leader of the free world.

Still, I was, of course, excited. When Obama's presidential victory was declared, the level of positive energy in the air was something I had never experienced before. Millions of people around the world celebrated the fact that racism in America had just been dealt a hefty blow. That night of celebration with the Obama family at Grant Park in Chicago was the beginning of a new era in American politics. It was motivation. "In the weeks following the election, I still wasn't sure if it was real or not," Nelson said.

I remember walking past my television set and seeing a press conference at the White House with the new president speaking. I had to pause for a second and look again. Having just elected an African American president for the first time took a while for me to get used to. But it was confirmation that a black man from the south side of anywhere in America could rise to the top, not just to become the leader of one of wealthiest nations in the world, but to be the leader of a company, a bank, or a law firm in America.

Not only did Obama win, twice, he served a full eight years in office without any major scandals or investigations into his administration, and he maintained the integrity of the office. But that's not to say the forces of racism didn't continue their work after his election. Over the eight years of his presidency, the level of disrespect and racist remarks aimed at the First Family was unprecedented. In a 2008 interview with

CNN, author Ronald Kessler talked about his book *In the President's Secret Service* and stated, "There were about three thousand threats a year under President [George W.] Bush, and now there are about twelve thousand. Of course, most of them are not credible, but they all have to be checked out." In 2007, then-US Senator Obama was immediately assigned Secret Service protection following the announcement of his candidacy for the presidency. This marked the earliest a candidate has ever received such protection.[66]

To the haters who professed to love America and yet attacked President Obama for his race, I ask, why was it such a struggle to accept a black president? Is it because a black man in the White House wasn't there to clean floors or serve caviar and champagne to visitors, as in our dark past? Seeing the bigoted and racist comments posted on social media about President Obama was another reminder of how close America still is to its racist past.

Donald Trump's victory in the 2016 presidential election wasn't a nightmare for all Americans. Trump winning the election was a dream come true for those opposed to equality among the races. Sadly, racism in America is embedded in the fiber of the land. It dates back to America's earliest days, and many of the policies and laws that exist today still adversely affect minorities in ways that no cross burning or Ku Klux Klan rally ever could. Donald Trump just pulled the scab off the wound that has never healed.

The 2017 presidential inauguration was a sad day for the descendants of black slaves in America who were so proud of their former commander in chief. The Obama family left the White House after their eight-year term, and many are wondering now, what have we gotten ourselves into? Since Trump has been in office, another provocative hashtag has gone viral on social media: #Resistance. It is emblematic of a campaign that calls for standing up to the oppressive practices of

---

66   Jeff Zeleny, "Secret Service Guards Obama, Taking Unusually Early Step," *New York Times*, May 4, 2007.

President Trump. But is Trump the real problem with America? When he is out of office, how many more Donald Trump–minded figures will be waiting in the wings to take his place?

———

"Voting rights was one of the most important parts of Martin's platform," Nelson said. "He knew that the only way that black people could have lasting and sustainable power in this country was through voting, and holding political offices at the federal, state, and local levels."

In 1966, Nelson ran for a seat on the Democratic Executive Committee in Montgomery, just after the passage of the Voting Rights Act of 1965. Nelson said that once the Voting Rights Act was passed, thousands of black Americans across the South registered to vote and the number of black people who either ran for office or became elected officials ballooned across the country. Nelson himself was one of the people who ran.

One of Rosa Parks's attorneys was a guy named Clifford Durr. He had previously worked under President Roosevelt's administration and after leaving Washington he came back to Alabama to retire. His wife was a woman named Virginia Durr, and they were a very powerful couple in Montgomery. One night I ran into them at a party, where we were all having a good time and enjoying the night. Out of the clear blue sky, Mrs. Durr leaned over to me and said, "Nelson, I want you to go down to the Montgomery Seed Store on Monday morning and tell the owner that you want to qualify to run for a seat on the Democratic Executive Committee. He's the chairman of the Democratic Party for the State of Alabama." To qualify to run for office, you had to go in front of the man and fill out the necessary paperwork, then he'd basically decide if you qualified or not.

Nelson told Mrs. Durr that he didn't know anything about the Democratic Executive Committee, and she said, "Don't worry, I will explain everything to you in detail, but later." Later that same night she told Nelson, "Do not tell the owner that I sent you down there, just tell him that you want to qualify to run for the Democratic Executive Committee."

All of this came out of nowhere. After the party that night we talked a little more, and then I went home. When I got home, I discussed it with my wife and she said that I should do it. The next morning, I got dressed in a clean suit and tie and nervously went over to the Montgomery Seed Store. When I walked into the store, I spotted two of my clients from the barbershop who were working there. I said, "I'm here to speak with the owner about running for office in Montgomery. Is he here?" They were very surprised.

When I walked into the office of the white owner, he was standing by his desk in a three-piece suit and wearing an expensive gold watch. I said, "Sir, my name is Nelson Malden, and I'd like to qualify to run for the Democratic Executive Committee in Precinct 2." He didn't give me any problems at all and simply went into his desk drawer and pulled out the paperwork, and I filled it out. That was it!"

In 1966, Nelson became the first African American in Montgomery to ever run for public office.

After I qualified, it was announced on the radio and in the newspaper that Nelson Malden was running for a seat on the Democratic Executive Committee. At the time, it was big news. Every person who walked into the barbershop received one of my campaign brochures. I told anyone who would listen to me that I was running for office and that they better vote for me on Election Day.

The day of the election was like one big party. My entire family came up from Pensacola and southern Alabama to support me, like I was running for president of the United States. We were in my house looking at the television the night the poll results came out. The white candidate who ran against me beat me by only five hundred votes, but I was happy with the outcome. My mother was so happy and proud that I stepped up and ran for office during a very critical time in America. There were a lot of people happy about me running, and then there were also a lot of people in Montgomery who were pissed that a black person ran for office, because it was unprecedented. The voting rights bill was just passed in 1965, so all of this was new for Montgomery.

———

The passage of the Voting Rights Act of 1965 was a major victory for the civil rights movement. It was a tremendous step forward at a time when a victory for the movement was desperately needed. By then, it was clearly understood that for blacks in America to gain the collective strength to foster significant changes in the policies that affected their lives, they would have to be able to wield power through voting. Following the assassination of President Kennedy in November 1963, blacks weren't sure of the direction the nation would go, having lost the civil rights movement's most powerful supporter. But two years later, the Voting Rights Act, signed by President Lyndon B. Johnson on August 6, 1965, was enacted to circumvent legal barriers that had become obstacles at the state and local levels for black voters attempting to exercise their right to vote in accordance with the Constitution's Fifteenth Amendment.

The first time I voted was sometime in the early sixties, and I remember that you had to first take a literacy test. There were sixty-five questions on the test, and the election official would ask you ten of those questions. If you answered some number of the ten questions wrong, you had to take the test over again, but they would not give you the same ten questions on your second try.

One of the questions would be something like, what does the US Constitution say about the square mileage of the District of Columbia? The answer was that the Constitution didn't say anything about the square mileage of the District of Columbia, or something to that effect. You understand what I'm saying? The test was designed for you to fail.

And the election officials had discretion over who would take the test and who wouldn't. If the election official happened to be a member of the KKK, then guess whom the tests were given to? And before the literacy test, there was the poll tax. The poll tax was basically a fee you paid before you could vote. There were a lot of obstacles in the way.

I've also heard that prospective black voters sometimes had to take a gumball test or a jellybean test to be able to register. The election officials put the candy in a jar, and you had to guess how many pieces were inside. If you answered wrong, you couldn't register.

The first time I voted, I felt like it was a great personal accomplishment. It was still a rare thing for black people in the South back then. When I went down to register to vote, there was a white woman sitting behind the desk and I was trying to be as polite to her as I possibly could. I was a little nervous that day because in the back of my mind I was thinking about all the black people who had been killed or lynched for trying to vote.

At that point, I had to ask Nelson: "King understood that for black people to gain political power in America we would have to use our voting power, so why has it been so difficult for us to be consistent in accomplishing that goal? Why have we had such a difficult time relaying that message to the African American community? Why is it that black people don't vote regularly?"

Nelson explained that in his view, one reason many African Americans don't exercise their right to vote is that many of us don't associate voting with progress in our lives. He said that we must associate our vote with some type of benefit. When we vote, some of us don't see the positive results of our vote, so consequently, we don't vote consistently. Without clear results, like more money in our bank account or more food on the table, people get discouraged.

"I get it," I said. "But what needs to be done to get more people out to vote? Look at all the blacks who came out to vote for Obama."

"There's not too much we can do besides continue to push forward," Nelson replied.

"We've tried just about everything that we can, but unless people understand how they can improve their lives through voting, I'm not sure what can be done. I'm not even sure that people today understand how the voting system works. How many people took a Civics 101 course in school and learned what the Electoral College is about and how it relates to their lives? This is an important issue to understand."

Maybe part of the problem is that people can't relate voting to other aspects of their lives.

———

Over the years, many black people have taken the right to vote for granted, while not taking into consideration the people who died and were brutalized for us to have this right. Neither Generation X nor millenials have had to fight for the right to vote. By the time we were born, the right to vote was a given. There are still obstacles, such as gerrymandering, which can make our vote count for less than it should, and there may soon be more obstacles, like voter ID laws, which would limit who can cast their votes; these aren't the types of obstructions, however, likely to lead to people getting killed. If we can vote without risk of injury, don't we owe it to our ancestors, and the generation who fought so hard to get us this right, to do so?

Part of what helped President Obama win was that minorities really turned out for him. In 2012, a record high of 66.6 percent of black people went to the polls.[67] This wasn't the same in 2016. In 2016, a record number of Americans voted, but black voter turnout fell to 59.6 percent.[68] I'm not certain how many more minority votes would have been necessary to keep Donald Trump from winning the presidency, but certainly Trump's rise to becoming president is the kind of thing that can happen when not enough citizens exercise our constitutional right to vote; not voting has consequences. I realized early on that if I didn't vote and Donald Trump won the election, I wouldn't have any right to complain about his policies, which could certainly make my life miserable.

I sometimes wonder if more black people would have gone to the polls if they'd known about racist things Trump has done over the years, like his involvement with the Central Park Five—when he took out a racially charged full-page ad in the *Wall Street Journal* making the case for the execution of five black teenagers accused of raping a New York City jogger, though it was later determined that the young men had nothing to do with the crime and they were released from prison—or if even this wouldn't have motivated them.

---

67   Jens Manuel Krogstad and Mark Hugo Lopez, "Black Voter Turnout Fell in 2016, Even as a Record Number of Americans Cast Ballots," Pew Research Center, May 12, 2017.

68   Ibid.

Participating in the election process can be an overwhelming task, especially when you're trying to maneuver through all the rhetoric and noise to figure out which candidate has the best policies. A few ways to wade through some of the minutiae are to simply go online and review the agenda of the candidate you're considering on their website, to read pamphlets containing information on the candidates, or to go to a campaign rally to listen to the candidate in person. The League of Women Voters is just one of the many nonpartisan groups that provide credible information on presidential candidates.

10: LEADERS AMONG US

I still remember when Rosa Parks was arrested on Montgomery Street. I was in the barbershop working the following day when a customer who knew her husband mentioned what happened on the bus. It was that same damn bus driver who she was having problems with before. The next day the incident was the talk of the town. Her action started the Montgomery Bus Boycotts.

On December 1, 1955, Rosa Parks was arrested for not giving up her seat on a public bus to a white passenger. The arrest was made in downtown Montgomery, about a mile and a half away from the College Hill Barbershop, where Nelson worked at the time.

"The bus driver messed with the wrong woman that night," Nelson said. Rosa Parks was the secretary at the local NAACP and she knew the city ordinances well. She knew the policies governing bus segregation in Montgomery better than the bus driver or the police. She knew that she was in the right that day when the driver told her to get out of the seat.

Parks's arrest was followed by a one-day bus boycott on her court date. However, to successfully challenge segregated public transportation, the NAACP knew it needed continued action. The new pastor at the local Dexter Avenue Baptist Church, Rev. Dr. Martin Luther King Jr., became the leader of the boycott and it lasted for 381 long days. King insisted on nonviolent action to achieve the goal of justice. "We must use the weapon of love," he said. In December 1956, the Supreme Court banned segregation on public transportation, and the boycott ended. It had been successful.[69]

Rosa Parks was the catalyst for what I think catapulted the civil rights movement. The murder of that boy Emmett Till was also a major contributor. Both gained nationwide attention in 1955, when the results of the US Supreme Court ruling in the Brown v. Board of Education *case, which had been decided a year earlier, were being felt around the country. This meant that the ground was fertile to push back hard against the system that had oppressed black people for years. It took activism and protests to bring about change.*

Nelson paused and turned to me, "I bet you didn't know that US Supreme Court Justice Thurgood Marshall was still just a young lawyer from Baltimore when he represented Oliver Brown in the *Brown v. Board of Education* case in '54."

He was just a struggling lawyer working for the NAACP before he won the Brown v. Board of Education *case, but the success of that case eventually led to desegregation of schools all over the South. The Brown case opened the door wide for the many cases that followed and were successful as well. It set a precedent, you understand? Florida, Mississippi, Alabama, South Carolina, and Arkansas—they all were under tremendous legal pressure to integrate their schools. All the states in the South didn't immediately desegregate, and in some cases, it took a few years, but this was significant, and it all started with a legal challenge by a black attorney from Baltimore.*

69   "Rosa Parks Was Arrested for Civil Disobedience, December 1, 1955," AmericasLibrary.com.

I had known that Thurgood Marshall was from Baltimore, but it's true that sometimes his importance to the civil rights movement doesn't register. Outside the legal world, I don't think we have appreciated Justice Marshall's accomplishments the way we should. Being the first African American appointed to the Supreme Court was a major accomplishment, especially in 1967. The airport in Baltimore is named after him, but sometimes I still feel like his legacy in Baltimore is an afterthought. Before Nelson mentioned it, I wouldn't have connected the dots between his life and the desegregation of schools. Ironically, Justice Marshall lived in West Baltimore, on Division Street. It's an area of the city I know very well, and yet I've rarely associated him with it. Today it has changed a lot, but it will always be his home.

Talking with Nelson, I began to understand that most of the civil rights heroes involved in the American civil rights movement were ordinary people before they began doing extraordinary things that changed the trajectory of America. Many of them were secretaries, preachers, lawyers, bus drivers, students, and the like. They were regular people who found themselves in positions where they could make a difference, and they did just that. The country was filled with young black men and women eager to step up when called upon to provide leadership and direction during a very challenging time. Some of them unwittingly became heroes by doing what they felt was the right thing to do. If it had not been for their courage and sacrifice, the movement would not have gained the traction it desperately needed throughout its course.

An example of black people who did a great service for the country during the civil rights era, but didn't get the respect and attention they were due for it—and there are many like this—are the Tuskegee Airmen. They were a group of African American men in the US Army Air Forces who were active in the military in the 1940s and 1950s. The airfield where they trained was in Tuskegee, Alabama, just minutes away from Montgomery and the Malden Brothers Barber-shop on Jackson Street; over the years, many of them were Nelson's regular customers.

Even though they put their lives on the line in service for their country, defending people of all colors, the airmen who visited the bar-bershop often talked about the racial discrimination they experienced in the military. According to Nelson, many of them talked openly in the barbershop about the racial insults and mistreatment they received from their white counterparts and superiors. Even when they were at war and flying dangerous missions over North Africa and Europe, black pilots were still not looked upon as equals in the military. The Tuskegee Airmen were willing to die for a country that they knew wouldn't die for them.

Some black activists were—and remain—highly controversial. When I asked Nelson his opinion on the Black Panthers, he agreed that they were "very controversial" but he also called them "extremely effective."

> *They were labeled extremists by the government and viewed as outlaws by some, but they still provided desperately needed support for struggling children and families. They did a lot of good supporting poor black communities in California and other places in the North. I have never felt or wished any ill will on anybody who wanted to support black people.*

———

Nelson's generation and the baby boomers had some of the most dynamic and charismatic leaders that America has ever known. They had King, of course, but they also had Ralph Abernathy, A. Philip Randolph, Rosa Parks, James Bevel, Medgar Evers, Malcolm X, Fred Hampton, Bayard Rustin, Hosea Williams, James Farmer, John Lewis,

Angela Davis, H. Rap Brown, Bobby Seale, Huey Newton—the list goes on. These generations developed social and political leaders who were willing not only to speak out, but also to put their lives on the line for a cause. And even after some were killed, courageous young men and women continued to step up to the plate.

I asked Nelson where the new young black leaders would emerge from, and he had some thoughts on the subject.

You have to start with getting the best students from the best colleges and universities. When you get the very best, you are going to come in first place. When the United States wanted to build a rocket that could go to the moon, but they didn't have the knowledge to do so, what did they do? They went out and found Wernher von Braun out of Germany, the engineer who was the best person educated in that area.

Education is the key to success. It's like a road map to solving almost any problem. If you have a good map of the territory, you can navigate it a lot better. But if you don't have a good map, you will get confused and you'll get lost. If you're in a car trying to drive from Montgomery, Alabama, back to Baltimore and you decide to take Route 80 West, you're going to end up in Texas. Education is the answer because it gives you the tools that you need to be successful. Most of those people you mentioned earlier had a good education, and that was the thing that helped them become good leaders.

In my experience with young people from here in Montgomery, I had a few customers who were outstanding students, very smart. One girl, MIT sent a special convoy to pick her up. I said, "Damn." She went to MIT and became an electrical engineer. The girl's father was a librarian at Alabama State, and his daughter had studied there with him. She received several offers for jobs from corporate America. Then another younger boy, Harvard sent for him, and he received an MD and MBA at the same time. Over the years, those were the type of customers I had, and most of them began as students at ASU.

Then there was my boy Lamar. I told him, "You know, Lamar, by the time you finish medical school, I'll be an old man. I want you to be my doctor." He says, "Yes sir, Mr. Nelson, I'm gonna take care of you." So, the last time I saw him, he came back to Montgomery on a company jet to attend his mother's birthday party, and I was invited. I saw him at the party and I said, "Lamar, what happened? I thought you were coming back when you finished medical school to take care of me." He laughed, then he looked at me and said, "Mr. Nelson, the corporate office made me an offer that I couldn't refuse." He worked for some huge pharmaceutical company in New York. When you're getting those types of opportunities, that's when you know that you've made it.

So, the answer to your question is simple. You must start first with the best students. They have the intellectual fortitude to become good leaders, but they also need good mentors to help them develop and mold them into good leaders. Most of the black leaders in my day were college educated and most had degrees. Education can be the strongest weapon a person can have if they use it the right way. Not just formal education, but a lifetime of education that produces deep thought and critical thinking. All the great leaders possessed those attributes.

Nelson often talked to me about the importance of leadership and how crucial it is for us to continue to cultivate the next generation of young leaders. He saw a vibrant young Dr. Martin Luther King Jr. in his prime and watched him as he evolved into one of the greatest leaders America has ever seen. Over the last few decades, we've had several competent African Americans emerge to captain the ship, but as we move into a new era of divisive politics and social justice, who will be the next generation of leaders with the skill set that can galvanize black America and take us to the next level?

"I believe that the next crop of young, bright African American chairmen and professors will be vast and plentiful," Nelson said.

I hope he's right.

11: KNOWLEDGE IS POWER

The time I spent in Alabama was invaluable, but afterward I still didn't feel like I was a person well versed in the golden era of the civil rights movement, and there were still big holes in my knowledge of black history. I had almost no understanding of the early years of African American history, when the first slave ships arrived in Britain's North American colony of Jamestown, Virginia, in 1619 from the Gold Coast, today the Republic of Ghana, filled with African slaves. I didn't know much about how African Americans, enslaved or free, soldiered through the two and a half centuries from their entrance into the United States to their emancipation: how they preserved their cultures, their spirits, and their willingness to fight for freedom, in spite of the best efforts of white Americans to destroy these. There are many important milestones within those four centuries that charted the course for black people in America, and I am still trying to learn about these.

King clearly understood the value of education. In much of his writing and many of his speeches he emphasized its importance. "The complete education gives one not only power of concentration, but worthy objectives upon which to concentrate."[70]

---

70   Martin Luther King Jr., "The Purpose of Education," *The Maroon Tiger* (Moorhouse College Student Newspaper), January–February 1947.

Nelson remembers how King dedicated his life to freedom and understood the role that education played in this fight, for himself as well as those around him.

It wasn't something that he took lightly. I still remember the time when Martin was extremely upset that he couldn't use the public library here in Montgomery to work on his doctoral dissertation because of segregation. Black people weren't allowed in the public library. I mean, he was really upset. I was still a student at Alabama State College at the time, so I suggested that he go to the college and use the library there.

Reverend King persevered and received his PhD in Systematic Theology from Boston University, adding "Doctor" to his name, and to what would soon be a long list of accomplishments.

Nelson's wife, Dee, has her own painful memories of America's educational system during the Jim Crow era of systemic segregation. She has always had an affinity for education and children, and from very early on in life she wanted to be a schoolteacher. She learned from her parents at a young age that a black person living in America needed to have an education because without it, their lives would be even more trying than they already were under the rule of Jim Crow. She was told that an education was the key to success, and she took this to heart, for herself and for others. After graduating from college in 1952, she earned a master's degree in elementary education from Alabama State College. Later that year, she began working in the segregated public-school system in Montgomery, Alabama, as a schoolteacher. It was her dream job.

In Montgomery, during the early years of the civil rights movement, Public Safety Day was a time when officers from the local police department visited area schools and gave presentations in front of a student audience about the work that the department conducted to help keep the community safe. It was billed as a public relations campaign designed to connect young people to law enforcement officials in a positive way, the equivalent of a visit from their local "Officer Friendly." Another goal of the effort was to cultivate in the students an interest in the department that might one day lead to their employment there. But the racism and degradation of people of color living in the South in those years was blatant, and it ran deep, deep enough to reach even the youngest of school-age children.

Because the public-school system was still racially segregated at the time, on Public Safety Day there were officers assigned to visit the students in the all-white schools and others assigned to visit the students in the all-black schools, like the one where Dee was a teacher. At the white schools, the visits were a pleasant and uplifting experience for the students, during which the officers spoke about the wholesome parts of their job—keeping order and helping others—and the possibility of a student having a career in the department one day.

In the black schools, the visits were a much different experience. In Dee's school as in other all-black schools, shackled and handcuffed black inmates who worked on a chain gang at the local prison were shepherded into the school auditorium and used as props in a presentation before elementary and junior high school students. "You don't want to end up like these niggas, do you, boys and girls? If not, you better straighten up," were the words "Officer Friendly" offered to the auditorium full of students who were trembling with fear. The students were traumatized by the suggestion that they too could end up in shackles and chains, like the black men who were paraded in front of them. The students spoken to weren't having disciplinary problems in class; they were run-of-the-mill students who performed well on tests and conducted themselves properly. They just happened to be black, and as such, they were treated in a dehumanizing way that contrasted with the public image of Public Safety Day.

Listening to Dee recount the story of how our must vulnerable commodity, our youth, had been intimidated and traumatized while in school angered me to my core. "It was shocking," she said. "This is how the police presented themselves to young students in Montgomery. So when they grew up with this fear of the police, it stayed with them as adults."

———

In the twenty-first century, the educational disparities between white students and students of color aren't quite as obvious as they used to be, but there are still plenty of them. During this journey to educate myself, I have tried to address two questions concerning African American history: how accurate is the information that's being taught in our schools, and how comprehensive is it?

I wonder what today's students are being taught about historic figures like Frederick Douglass, an escaped slave and abolitionist leader, Harriet Tubman, an escaped slave who helped others escape through the Underground Railroad, and Sojourner Truth, an escaped slave, abolitionist, and women's rights activist, as well as more recent leaders like Adam Clayton Powell Jr., a black congressman from Jim Crow–era New York who was elected to Congress, the great Rev. Dr. Martin Luther King Jr., and US Supreme Court Justice Thurgood Marshall.

The stories of African American men and women who had the will to succeed against all odds are important for young people to hear, and not just in February, but every day.

Young people hold the key to the future of America because they will be the leaders of our nation. They will be the politicians who make the laws that reflect what our country values. They will be our policemen, teachers, scientists, and engineers. The things they're learning in school today are vital, including African American history. Education is capable of instilling in them an awe and appreciation for the struggles of the past that they can use to contextualize where we are today and help propel our country forward; if this falls by the wayside, we may become stagnant or even regress. Making African American history a substantial part of the curriculum of our education system must be a priority. Education can also conquer racism, or prevent it before it begins.

Not long ago, I ran into a friend of mine, Marisol Johnson, who was an active member of the Baltimore County School Board through October 2017. We spoke about the changes that need to be made to our students' curriculum to better educate them on African American history. She agreed that using the current curriculum is a disservice to students of all colors and to the future of our country. She also spoke from personal experience of seeing how this particularly hurts African American children, who become accustomed to learning about white heroes, and very infrequently about ones who look like them. She spoke about how this can shape a student's opinion of what he or she is capable of, and what kinds of contributions the student might be able to make to our world.

We need a curriculum in place that expands the amount of time our students spend reading and writing about African American history, but also, importantly, the time they spend discussing it. Students should be encouraged to ask questions about it, and about current racial issues too. They should have the freedom to debate, to engage others in a way beneficial to the knowledge and growth of all students. This could initially seem awkward because talking about race can be considered taboo, but we need to stop being afraid to say the words "black," "white," "race," and "segregation." Without open dialogue, problems and misunderstandings are swept under the rug; knowledge isn't furthered. As King said, "Education must enable one to sift and weigh evidence, to discern the true from the false, the real from the unreal, and the facts from the fiction."[71]

Additionally, despite the landmark ruling in *Brown vs. Board of Education*, our students have continued to be racially isolated for decades. Marsisol said that Baltimore County schools are particularly segregated, but segregation is a problem nationwide. When we deny our students the opportunity to meaningfully engage with others who have different backgrounds, we're not preparing them—white or minority—for tomorrow. To see that we're still having conversations in 2018 about desegregating our schools is disheartening, and it sometimes seems that for action to be taken, we must point out that a lack of diversity is hurting white kids; pointing out that it's hurting black kids can be insufficient. Still, we must not get jaded; we must continue to push for progress. Our children and the future of our country are at stake.

Marisol said that beyond the problems resulting from the lack of interracial engagement is the problem of how schools that predominantly serve children of color tend to have fewer qualified teachers, simply because of turnover. She said that these schools also generally have fewer resources, such as books and computers, and this pattern is repeated constantly all over the country.

In the midst of day-to-day battles to overcome curriculum issues, discipline issues, and a host of other challenges, it can be hard for education officials to see the big picture, how these challenges came to be in the first place. Marisol believes that there's a common assumption that white people are choosing to live in white neighborhoods and black families are choosing to live in black neighborhoods, and they're choosing the schools that their children go to accordingly. But this assumption doesn't consider why black families often have to stay in certain neighborhoods, even if the schools there aren't good

---

71   King, "The Purpose of Education."

for their children. It doesn't consider the factors that make moving to neighborhoods with better schools prohibitive for many black families, such as mortgage redlining, zoning issues, and other forms of housing discrimination, as well as the wage gap between the races, things that still determine the makeup of neighborhoods today.

Betsy DeVos, the US Secretary of Education, made the outlandish claim that HBCUs were pioneers of school choice. Secretary DeVos seemed completely unaware that African Americans didn't have much of a choice of what school to go to when HBCUs opened; they were refused entry into schools that enforced segregation or were only interested in white students. Her push for "school choice" today continues to dismiss what is in reach of African American students.[72]

Another issue in schools that predominantly serve children of color is the disciplinary practices that set children up for a lifetime of being subject to institutional correction. Marisol told me about so-called "zero-tolerance" policies that aim to lessen discipline issues by subjecting students to harsh consequences for minor infractions, as well as on the very first instance of more significant ones, brand children as troublemakers with no margin for error, and begin the process of setting them up to fail in the school system, which in turn sets them up for failure in society. She said that the Baltimore County School Board is debating a discipline policy under which, if a student gets suspended, the suspension could stay on their record all the way through their senior year of high school, and could even be included on a student's college transcript.

Just as in adulthood, where there are sentencing disparities between white and minority criminal offenders, even for the same crime, children of color in our school systems are disciplined more frequently and more harshly than their white counterparts. Today's

---

72 Maya Rhodan, "The Secretary of Education Equated Historically Black Colleges to 'School Choice,'" *Time*, February 28, 2017.

discipline reformers are promoting programs such as restorative justice interventions as alternatives to suspending students.[73] In Baltimore County, black female students are being suspended or disciplined at a disproportionately higher rate than any other subgroup, even more often than black males.[74] We often talk about the school-to-prison pipeline, but we're just perpetuating and making that pipeline even more effective with these types of draconian policies.

It wasn't until about five years ago that Baltimore County began to make real changes in its school administration. The county hired a young black male superintendent, who brought in deputies who, for the most part, were people of color. Marisol said the school board began having courageous conversations about race and the difference between equality and *equity*, which in education means that the idea that equality, or treating everyone exactly the same, might not actually produce educational justice in a system where students of color had been dramatically left behind in the first place. Now they're able to make some changes—slow changes, but important ones—in the curriculum and in equity in the system. Baltimore County now writes its own curriculum. It makes an honest attempt not just to talk about African American history during African American History Month but to sprinkle in some of those facts throughout the school year. Recently, the county has changed its reading assignments to gear them toward stories that are more culturally relevant to their student population.

The disparities between white and minority students that persist in public education are issues that we often don't talk about on the systemic level; we're won't talk about them on a school-based level, because they start at the top. For far too long we have allowed people who don't look like us to make decisions for our minority students.

73   Tom Loveless, "Racial Disparities in School Suspensions," 2017 Brown Center Report, March 24, 2017.

74   Lauren Camera, "Black Girls Are Twice as Likely to Be Suspended, In Every State," *US News & World Report*, May 9, 2017.

When we don't talk about the different educational outcomes for different groups of students—for students of color, LGBTQ students, and particularly those who fall into both categories—we are doing our children a major disservice. What I clearly understand now is that diversity in leadership and among our decision makers is critical, because many of the people who are in those positions today are either blind to their biases or don't have our kids' best interests at heart. Some of them never did.

12: WOMEN WHO LEAD

Though they do not always receive the recognition they deserve, many women played prominent roles in the civil rights movement. These unsung heroes marched in the protests and bravely stood on the front lines, where they were often verbally abused and sometimes physically attacked by the opposition. Many were arrested and spent time in prison, or were critically injured during clashes with law enforcement officials. These were women like Fannie Lou Hamer, who worked as a voting-rights activist, primarily in the volatile state of Mississippi, where black voters had been systematically disenfranchised for decades and racially motivated killings of blacks were a common occurrence.

Septima Poinsette Clark was a teacher and leader in the Charleston, South Carolina chapter of the NAACP, who designed workshops and courses to help blacks who wanted to register to vote pass the required literacy test, as well as how to complete important forms like driver's license exams She was an unsung hero who understood the role education could play in helping people fight for their rights, pursue their dreams, and have different perspectives toward the world around them.[75]

---

75 Wu Xinyun, "Black Women in American Civil Rights Movement." Women Study Discussion Group, 2001:5. Web, November 17, 2013.

Hazel Gregory was another unsung hero working behind the scenes. She was the secretary for the Montgomery Improvement Association, the organization that spearheaded the Montgomery Bus Boycott, and she worked directly with King. She was a friend and mentor to many of the college students in Montgomery who were eager to participate in the movement. She was also a regular customer of the Malden Brothers Barbershop who would normally come in to get a trim and a shape-up. "Mrs. Gregory was a very fashionable and attractive woman, but she was also very bright and business savvy. She had two children and a husband who was a bellhop at one of the white hotels downtown," Nelson recalls.

It wasn't just her skills but her spirit that set Hazel Gregory apart as a leader. "Mrs. Gregory was one of the strongest and most coura-geous women I ever met," Nelson says of her now. "She was fearless." According to a story circulated by the locals, Mrs. Gregory on one occasion assembled a convoy of hearses from the local black-owned funeral homes to rescue several injured protesters from the bus sta-tion in Montgomery. Some of them had been severely beaten by an angry white mob and needed immediate medical attention, but they were trapped inside the bus terminal. After putting out the call, Mrs. Gregory went down to the station and helped place the injured in the hearses, alleviating their suffering through her quick thinking and willingness to roll up her sleeves and get to work.

With so much to do in a time of turmoil and confusion, there could be some harrowing moments. Hazel Gregory was a very busy woman, and she was usually juggling several different responsibilities for the Montgomery Improvement Association. Nelson remembers that one day Mrs. Gregory came to the barbershop to get her hair cut, which she normally did every couple of weeks. When she arrived at the shop that evening, she placed her belongings on a chair by the window and seated herself in the barber chair. When she got out of the chair, she paid Nelson, grabbed her purse, and ran out of the door to get to another meeting. It wasn't until later that night that Nelson spotted some writing tablets that someone had left behind, but he had no idea who they belonged to. "We'd had several customers coming in and out of the barbershop that day. I asked my brothers, Spurgeon and Stephen, if they knew who the items belonged to, and they also didn't know."

Nelson began looking through one of the tablets for information to aid him in identifying the owner. "That's when I saw writing that said, 'Meeting Minutes' and 'Strategy for White House Meetings.' There were some other notations that read, 'Parliamentary Procedures and Robert's Rules of Order.'"

The notepads were the recorded meeting minutes for a Montgomery Improvement Association board meeting that, according to the dates, had recently been conducted with King, Ralph Abernathy, and the other members of the association. Mrs. Gregory had mistakenly left the materials behind in the barbershop in her rush to get to her next meeting on time. "There was a lot of other information there that I'd rather not talk about," Nelson says. "Let's just say this—if those writings had landed in the wrong hands, that could have been a major problem! After I realized what they were and whom they belonged to, I called Mrs. Gregory at home."

"I said, 'Mrs. Hazel, this is Nelson Malden. I think I have some writing pads that belong to you. You left them here when you came in earlier.' And she said, 'Oh my God, Nelson, I was in here having a heart attack. I thought I lost them. Thank you, thank you, thank you.' We were about to close, so I dropped them off at her home."

Throughout the long years of the movement, women worked in leadership roles in all the major civil rights organizations: the NAACP, SNCC, Congress of Racial Equity, Urban League, SCLC, and many more. They sacrificed their time, families, and lives, and without their hard work and courage, the movement would not have been successful.

Today as much as back then, making progress in the movement for black lives requires all hands on deck, and activist and founder of the black feminist movement Alice Walker, First Lady Michelle Obama, US Senator Kamala Harris, activist and Women's March on Washington co-chair Tamika Mallory, and Congresswomen Maxine Waters, founders of Black Lives Matter Alicia Garza, Patrisse Cullors and Opal Tometi, Barbara Lee, Eleanor Holmes Norton, Terri Sewell, Karen Bass, and Frederica Wilson are among the many black women who raise powerful voices for racial justice in America. Many more such women come from the world of entertainment, like Oprah Winfrey, Viola Davis, and Cathy Hughes.

———

The women who lead us also help us focus and think about the world in a different way. They can light a fire in our bellies, inspiring us all to take action to make the world a better place. In 2015, civil rights activist Bree Newsome became my WCW—that's "women crush Wednesday," for those of you who aren't tuned into social-media acronyms. Back on June 27, 2015, Brittany Ann "Bree" Newsome was arrested and charged with defacing a monument after she climbed a thirty-foot-tall flagpole in Columbia, South Carolina, to remove the Confederate flag that flew in front of the statehouse. Instantly I became a fan of her efforts, and I was proud to see a black woman so bold that the whole world was watching her and (frequently) cheering her on.

When I asked Bree what prompted her to go to Columbia to rip down the flag that has become a symbol of hate to so many, she had an interesting answer. She stated that after the June 17, 2015 massacre in Charleston, South Carolina, in which nine church members and the pastor at Emanuel African Methodist Episcopal Church were killed, she was compelled to do something. Calls to remove the Confederate flag dramatically intensified in the wake of the bloodshed. After the shooter, Dylann Roof, confessed that his motivation for the killings was an attempt to start a race war in America, even South Carolina's Republican governor, Nikki Haley, joined in the sea of voices that thought that it was finally time to remove the flag. Yet many more political leaders unabashedly continued to support this racist symbol, or were still paralyzed by indecision or disinterest.

One thing that is important to understand about South Carolina is that it was the heart of the Confederacy. South Carolina was the first state to secede from the union during the Civil War. And much of the wealth that made Charleston into an elegant city that attracts millions of tourists each year stemmed directly or indirectly from the slave trade. The ancestors of most of the black people in this country who are descended from enslaved people came through the Port of Charleston. In 2000, the state had moved the Confederate flag from the dome of the statehouse to the lawn. It was a compromise, but no one could mistake the underlying message: "We're not taking this flag down."

Bree had always been aware of the problem of the Confederate flag in the South. Half of her father's family is from North Carolina, and her mother's family is from South Carolina. Even though she attended grade school in Maryland, not far from Baltimore, she spent most of her life in North and South Carolina. She had seen firsthand how the flag that some white Southerners claimed was only a representation of "heritage" could be used to frighten and oppress blacks. In 2014, Bree was living in Charlotte, North Carolina, where she had a conversation with another activist who was from Rock Hill, in South Carolina. They both said that if they ever had the opportunity to take down the flag in Columbia, which seemed to officially endorse the views of white supremacists, they would personally take that risk.

Bree had been arrested once before—while participating in a voting-rights sit-in in Raleigh, North Carolina, after the state passed a voter suppression bill—and she felt that removing the flag was a cause that would be worth a second trip through the legal system.

But the massacre was a precipitating point for her. "I was a grassroots community organizer in Charlotte, North Carolina, and Charleston is just four hours away, so there was no reason why something like what happened in the church couldn't happen in a church near where I lived."

For decades, white supremacists had been attacking black churches, civil rights protests, and social justice workers. To see that level of violence in the church was shocking, but she recognized that it was nothing new—nor would it be the last incident of its kind. She told me that her mind certainly didn't immediately go to the Confederate flag at that point. What she found personally offensive at first was the way that sequence of events played out: "You had this horrible massacre at the church, obviously a racially motivated crime. The immediate response from South Carolina government officials was, 'Are black people going to be violent?'" Then as Bree explained it, the focus promptly shifted to the Confederate flag in Columbia, which had been controversial since it was first raised in 1961 as a response to the civil rights movement, almost a century after the end of the war that the flag's supporters wanted to honor. There was never any doubt about what the flag represented. And South Carolina's refusal to lower the flag to half-staff when they were burying the victims of the church shooting, one of whom, Clementa Pinckney, was a member of the South Carolina Senate, was extremely offensive to Bree.

Bree has ancestors who were enslaved in South Carolina and she knows their names: Theodore and Minerva Diggs. They were held in bondage on a plantation in Milford, South Carolina, at the time of the Civil War. Bree is descended from their youngest child, their first child to be born into freedom. She also has a great uncle who was lynched in Goldsboro, North Carolina, so for her civil rights and social justice are very personal issues. Her grandmother, who grew up in Greenville, South Carolina, in the 1920s, spent a lot of time with Bree and would tell her about her own experiences with the Ku Klux Klan. From a very early age, these things and her experience of being descended from people who lived through those trying days in the South were a part of Bree's world.

So there were a lot of reasons why Bree made the decision to act, to put herself in the position of risking not only arrest but quite possibly her life. Her greatest concern was not so much the police as it was someone coming at her with a gun or some other kind of deadly weapon. One reason why she acted so early in the morning, was that there was a Ku Klux Klan rally planned at that site later in the day. She also wanted her actions to stand in contrast to those of Dylann Roof, who went to Charleston under cover of night and killed elderly black women and black men in a sanctuary while they were praying. In the tradition of old school civil rights and civil disobedience, Bree decided that she was going to do what she did out in broad daylight, for anyone to see.

When I asked Bree what her feelings were on the morning she took the flag down, her response surprised me. "The first word that comes to mind for me is 'trauma,' and not just my trauma and not just the history of trauma in my family, but the trauma of our people." And that's part of what she wanted to symbolize. She wanted others to visualize a black woman scaling the pole and unhooking the Confederate flag. It was a choice that made sense, but that didn't make it an easy choice. During the entire time of planning her action, Bree went through different mental and emotional states. In the days leading up to June 27, she endured both waves of fear and waves of feeling really emboldened.

In the end, not everyone was supportive of Bree's decision to strike a direct blow for justice.

I think this is the way that it's always been, the same way it was during the civil rights movement. Martin Luther King Jr. spoke many times about the subject. You have folks who are unabashedly racist. . . . I think that most are either unaware of the facts surrounding the issue or they're indifferent. That's one of the things that King spoke about, especially in Birmingham, of how the real issue was not the Ku Klux Klan, but it's the silence of white moderates. The problem is the people who really don't want to shake things up too much. . . . Things might have to get a little uncomfortable before they get better. Then, in the black community, it's kind of a similar situation. You have the people who are more radical and who are about black reparations. And then you have the people who are kind of moderate and believe we're making progress, so let's not rile things up.

The hard truth of being a leader in the fight for civil rights is that no matter how right an action looks when we look back at it, the reality is that not everyone—sometimes not even the people we expect will be on our side—will support it in the moment. Not everyone in the black community was supportive of the sit-ins, marches, and other actions black activists and their allies took back in the 1960s. Today, there's a lot of revisionist history concerning the civil rights movement. Suddenly, with the weight of history on their side, everyone was with King back then and everybody was willing to march to the bridge in Selma. But at the time, that wasn't how it really was. That's why the leadership of women like Bree Newsome, today, just as much as fifty years ago, is so important. Their courageous actions not only move the conversation forward directly, they remind us all that sometimes boldness and a willingness to take personal risks, with or without the approval of those around us, are required to serve the cause of justice.

13: IN THE END

Imagine yourself sitting in a black-owned barbershop today, full of black men and boys debating current events. They may be talking about the NFL players kneeling during the national anthem, the latest unarmed black person shot by police, body cameras, Black Lives Matter, or Donald Trump's latest antics or tweets. Maybe they're remembering the time he called the white supremacists in the Charlottesville, Virginia protest "good people" or when he called African nations, as well as Haiti and El Salvador, "shithole" countries. Maybe they're speaking about the backlash from individual countries, the fifty-five–nation African Union, and the people and companies throughout the United States who spoke out against Trump's description. Or maybe they're enjoying listening to the stories of the elderly man who walks in from time to time and begins telling stories about the days of old—every black barbershop has one of these men.

Today, black men converse about anything, whenever and wherever they choose, unlike in Nelson's time, when the barbershop was one of the few places this occurred. The lively feel of the black barbershop, as a place to share ideas and to debate, what the Nelson Brothers Barbershop had, still exists today.

During the several days I spent in Montgomery, absorbing the culture of the city, eating fried green tomatoes and peach cobbler, and engulfing my spirit in the soul of the South, my perception of the civil rights movement dramatically altered. Now I see it in an entirely different, brighter light. I have a clear picture of what really occurred in those years and how they connect to the challenges of today. Before I met Nelson, I was aware of the highly publicized events that occurred back then, like Bloody Sunday, the March on Washington, King's assassination, Emmett Till's murder, Rosa Parks's arrest, and others, but I was blind to their substance and interconnection, and how they affected history. I had a distorted view of the movement that was obscured by ignorance, a lack of respect for the past, and intellectual laziness. But then I developed a friendship with an eighty-four-year-old man from Alabama who lived through those years and enlightened me in ways that I had never thought possible.

Nelson became a bottomless source of information for me. He knew that young black men and women had been lynched in the South for decades, not only by the Ku Klux Klan but also by mobs of otherwise ordinary white people. He knew of African American church members whose sanctuaries were torched in Alabama, Georgia, and Mississippi by white supremacists bent on dismantling the movement. That was during a period when it was relatively easy to terrorize a black person in America. Hate crimes and domestic terrorism were almost never prosecuted, and even when they were, obtaining a conviction in a court of law was rarer still.

For most of my life, I didn't see the big picture of the complex journey African Americans have taken, from when they were brought into this country as slaves, to modern times. Since then I've learned of things I was misinformed about, and thought time again about how I hadn't appreciated our resilience as a people—how no matter what we've had to endure, we are still here and we are still strong. I believe this to be true of the generations before me, and also Generation Xers and millennials. Many of us have struggled to understand and appreciate our history, and because of this we've suffered. Many of us have never fully understood who we are because a big part of our history has been missing from our lives.

The names of civil rights icons don't always resonate with us today, and many of us couldn't reference anyone besides Martin Luther King Jr. We don't know much about the activists' courage, the sacrifices they made, and how they put their lives on the line to stamp out the oppressive laws that robbed blacks of their civil liberties. Over the years I only knew the bare minimum about the Emmett Till case. I didn't know that he was only fourteen years old when he was violently murdered. I had no idea that Rosa Parks was forced to move to Detroit, Michigan, after the Montgomery Bus Boycott because of the threats to her life, and that she was blackballed from employment in Montgomery. I had no idea that Medgar Evers was with the NAACP in Mississippi, where he was assassinated outside his house by the Ku Klux Klan. I was unaware of the Dred Scott decision of 1857 that denied the citizenship of slaves and even of African Americans. I'd heard of the 1963 Birmingham church bombing many times, but I didn't know important details of the tragedy, like the names of the four young black girls who were killed in the explosion: Addie Mae, Denise McNair, Carole Robertson, and Cynthia Wesley.

After I dove into the history of the American civil rights movement, I learned how it was a turning point not just for this country, but for the entire world, because the world was watching America to see whether it would live up to its own stated ideals. During the 1960s, the movement was the most pressing domestic issue on the agenda of Congress and the president. While America was attempting to boost its image as a superpower in the world, other countries had deep concerns about the domestic issues the United States government was struggling to manage. The government was under pressure to look in the mirror and decide: are these images of people being brutalized by police the images we want to be defined by to the rest of the world?

Many politicians were also concerned about their own personal legacies and wanted to be on the right side of history, just as they do today. While we're having public discussions about things like the removal of Confederate flags and Confederate monuments, every politician is faced with the choice: to be on the right side of history, or be remembered as being on the side of the neo-Nazis and white nationalists who rallied in Charlottesville, Virginia, and other parts of the nation. Understanding these pressures on political figures, which are as real today as they were in the 1950s and 1960s, is the key to devising strategies that can help justice and kindness win over ignorance and hatred.

I've learned a lot in recent years, but I'm not a historian or an expert on the life and legacy of Rev. Dr. Martin Luther King Jr. and the civil rights movement. I'm a layman who met a barber from Montgomery who turned out to be a walking encyclopedia of knowledge. By the time Nelson finished opening my eyes to the truth, I was in one of those mental spaces where most people never want to be, like, *Did I just see what I thought I saw?* Knowing what I know now, it's impossible for me to un-ring that bell and act like those historic atrocities aren't disturbing, because the way black people were treated in America back then was unconscionable. This change has made me unable to look away when I see similar crimes committed against humanity today. I know too many stories of how ordinary people back then took what they had—a simple conviction that what they were seeing was wrong—and used it to bring about massive civil rights victories.

Today I want to shout from the rooftops everything I know about how African Americans as a people stay strong. I want to shout to all the old-school activists and marchers who put their lives on the line for me, for us, for my daughter and the children she'll have. I want to shout to the teachers across the country educating our students the right way, with the right history, to the school activists and student advocates in the trenches, fighting the good fight; to the civil liberties soldiers on the front lines in Birmingham, Baltimore, Charlottesville, Charleston, Chicago, Dallas, Detroit, Ferguson, Houston, Los Angeles, New York, and other cities around the globe. I want to shout a thank-you to my middle-school teacher Mr. Thomas for slapping me upside the head for being chronically late for class and explaining to me why a black man can never be late for anything, even when I didn't understand. And I want to shout to the slave owners turning over in their graves because their worst nightmare came true: President Barack Hussein Obama.

Many of us who were born after the death of Dr. Martin Luther King Jr. believe that the racism and hatred we experience today is equivalent to the racism and hatred experienced generations before us, but I don't believe that's the case. The racism that our ancestors experienced was brutal, normalized, and deeply entrenched in every walk of American life, for centuries. There were laws and policies to enforce the demeaning treatment of people of color. Many Southerners wanted ethno-nationalism, in which America would be defined by one ethnic trait: whiteness. Undoubtedly, there are still challenges for us to tackle, but when I hear comments like, "We've come a long way" about race relations in America, they no longer sound like a cliché to me. I know so much more now about the distance we've traveled, and the costs of the journey.

This country has a brutal and unjust track record, and the work that still needs to be done will not be easy. Bree Newsome, the young activist who was arrested for climbing a flagpole to remove a Confederate flag in front of the South Carolina statehouse, once said to me that in her view, the civil rights movement wasn't just a movement about *civil* rights, it was also about *human* rights. There was a time in America when blacks were classified as second-class humans, inferior to the white race. That's the type of ideology that King and other civil rights leaders had to contend with.

America is still one big melting pot of different cultures, races, and ethnicities living together under one constitution: Asians, Native Americans, Latinos, African Americans, whites, and others, all chasing the American dream. We coexist in a mélange of different hues, but the playing field still isn't level. What can be done today to create more diversity, to establish equity and inclusion for minorities? The keys to accomplishing these goals include policy changes, but changes in attitudes are also required.

How can our society put the next generation in a position to be successful? Subjects that I often think about are the effects of generational wealth, or poverty, and leaving behind a legacy that can help my children flourish. I believe that most people think about these things at some point, but having the ability to accomplish their goals is a different matter. Access to a quality education, jobs, and a *livable* wage, not a minimum wage, must be our focus. In our conversations, Nelson mentioned to me that just before King was killed, he began to speak often and publicly about economic injustice and inequality in America. He knew that without secure jobs and consistent income, it would be difficult for African Americans to find the strength to fight for their rights.

There are many ways each of us can help carry the movement for black lives and equality forward—like taking part in the new civil rights movement, marching in the streets, fighting for economic justice, voting and helping others to vote, supporting and lifting up the people around us who make sacrifices to be in this fight on our behalf. But all of these actions start from the same place: learning about African American history and educating others about it. I am so grateful every day for having been given the life-changing opportunity to become friends with Nelson Malden, a chronicler of the American civil rights movement and a living embodiment of all that blacks have fought to attain for hundreds of years. I hope that reading this book can pass on to others some portion of the gift that Nelson has given to me, and I hope the actions I take with the knowledge I've gained from our friendship are worthy of the legacy that he and the many other men and women have created for my generation and those that will come after.

14: MURDER IN MEMPHIS

Thursday, April 4, 1968, started out as another normal day inside the Malden Brothers Barbershop. The barbershop was filled for most of the day with students from Alabama State and middle-aged men hoping to get a haircut before the weekend began. In most barbershops, Friday and Saturday are the busiest days of the week, so it's often a good idea to go on a Thursday, to get into your favorite barber's chair before the weekend rush begins.

But, on that day, 338 miles northwest of Montgomery, a tragedy of astronomical proportions was taking shape in Memphis, Tennessee.

By 1968, Martin Luther King Jr. had become a Nobel Peace Prize winner and world-renowned advocate of civil rights and human rights. He was recognized almost anywhere he travelled in America. He was celebrated and disliked, and one of the most talked-about black Americans of all time. His work had made him the leader of the American civil rights movement.

On April 3, King and his entourage of trusted men had arrived in Memphis to support the protests and demonstrations of the city's black sanitation workers, who were on strike. King was there to support the people and to stand shoulder to shoulder with them on the right side of justice. He was also scheduled to speak at the Mason Temple

Church of God in Christ, where he would deliver his final speech. Many people who had heard King give speeches over the years would later say that this was the most powerful speech he had ever given. It's known as "I've Been to the Mountaintop."

On April 4, at approximately six p.m., James Earl Ray fired a single bullet from his gun, striking King in the right side of his face while he was standing on the balcony outside his motel room at the Lorraine Motel in Memphis, Tennessee. The civil rights icon died within minutes.

"It was almost closing time, and I was cutting a customer's hair when the phone rang, and another customer answered it," Nelson recalls.

> *He was only on the phone for a split-second before he dropped the receiver and began yelling, "They shot Martin. They shot Martin, he's dead." He was traumatized. I was in shock too and could barely speak, but I said to the guy, "Are you sure? Are you sure?"*

> *He responded by saying, "Yes. They shot him up in Memphis, and he's dead."*

> *The customer who was in my barber chair at the time getting his hair cut began weeping and almost fell out of the chair and onto the floor. There were a few other people in the shop that night, and they began to cry and yell. It was a terrible scene.*

Nelson had first met King fourteen years before, in 1954, when the reverend was only twenty-five years old, long before the world would come to know him. Nelson remained King's regular barber until 1960, when King moved his family from Montgomery to Atlanta. But even after he moved away, he frequently returned to Montgomery, and each time he did, he went to Jackson Street to get a haircut and catch up with his favorite barber.

"To me, Reverend King wasn't just a civil rights leader, he was also a friend, and it's always tough when you lose a friend. Even though we believed that he could be killed at any time, it was still a shock to us all. It was a terrible time."

Political and community leaders were concerned that after King's assassination mass rioting would erupt around the country, which could lead to serious injuries and death. Unfortunately for the nation, those fears came true. Rioting and looting broke out in sixty-two cities from coast to coast.[76] The rampage left thirty-nine people dead, twenty-one thousand arrested, and more than twenty-six hundred injured, and was responsible for damages estimated at $65 million.[77]

The mayor of Chicago issued a very stark directive to law enforcement officials there: Mayor Richard J. Daley later told reporters that he had ordered police "to shoot to kill any arsonist or anyone with a Molotov cocktail in his hand . . . and . . . to shoot to maim or cripple anyone looting any stores in our city."[78] In the first two days of rioting, police reported numerous civilian deaths but were unable to determine whether they were caused by the riots or other crimes. No official death toll was given for the tragedy, although published accounts say nine to eleven people died during the rioting. Three hundred fifty people were arrested for looting, and one hundred sixty-two buildings were destroyed by arson. Bulldozers moved in to clean up after the riots, leaving behind vacant lots that are still empty decades later.[79]

According to Nelson, there were no riots, protests, or demonstrations in Montgomery after the assassination. He says the city was

76 *Time* Staff, "Time Looks Back: The Assassination of Martin Luther King, Jr.," *Time*, April 4, 2013.

77 *Newsweek* Archives, "Photos: The Rampage That Came After Martin Luther King Jr. Was Slayed," *Newsweek*, January 16, 2017.

78 James Coates, "Riots Follow Killing of Martin Luther King," *Chicago Tribune*, 2017.

79 Ibid.

quiet and somber. "Many of us were still in shock and didn't feel the need to lash out that way because we knew Martin personally and we knew that wouldn't be something that he would have wanted."

A few days after King was assassinated, there was a viewing and memorial service for him in Memphis at the R. S. Lewis Funeral Home. One of the employees of the funeral home had been at the Lorraine Motel when the assassination occurred, and he supposedly chased after the shooter. The next day, a private funeral was held in Atlanta, followed by another public service.

I remember that day well. The skies were clear, and the sun was shining most of the day. It was almost like God was sending us a message, saying that everything would be fine.

Nelson, his brother Stephen, and some friends drove to Atlanta that morning at about six a.m. Nelson said there was a lot of traffic on the roads, so it was good that they'd left early. "By the time we got to Atlanta that morning, thousands of people were already there on the streets, waiting for the services to begin," Nelson said.

"After the private funeral service with his family and invited guests at Ebenezer Baptist Church, his casket was carried out of the church and placed on the back of an old wagon that was pulled by two mules."

"Mules?" I asked.

"Yes."

The two mules carried King's body and casket through the streets of Atlanta as a procession of thousands of people followed behind them to a second memorial service. The procession was three miles, from Ebenezer Baptist Church to the campus of Morehouse College, of which King was an alumnus.

There were important people everywhere, walking with the crowd of mourners through the streets of Atlanta. Bobby Kennedy and his wife, Ethel Kennedy, were there, along with the legendary [singer] Harry Belafonte, [writer] James Baldwin, [actor] Sidney Poitier, and many other Hollywood celebrities and entertainers.

But I remember how quiet it was that day as we walked the streets. It was one of the most somber days I'd ever experienced. Thousands of people were there, and in the beginning, other than some occasional cries and whimpering off in the distance, no one made a sound. There were thousands of people everywhere, but it was so quiet you could hear a pin drop. Then someone started singing "We Shall Overcome," and it spread like wildfire across the crowd.

Nelson says that the memorial service started sometime in the afternoon, and that the president of Morehouse, Benjamin Mays, and Ralph Abernathy were two of the speakers. "Martin and Abernathy founded the Southern Christian Leadership Council together and were very close. They were like brothers. He said some real kind words about the life that Martin led and the work he had done to make a difference in the world."

Nelson also described how the service was held outside, because there were far too many people to fit in any indoor venue.

You could see the pain in people's eyes all day long, all the way up until that point. But then later, after the memorial service at Morehouse, the tide shifted, and it felt festive, in a strange way. People started singing, and some were even dancing in the streets. Suddenly, the mood was joyful and pleasant. Although a man had been killed, assassinated, which was a tragedy for America, people began to celebrate his great life and accomplishments.

He had accomplished more in his thirty-nine years on this earth than most people will ever do living a full life. That says a lot.

I could see pain in Nelson's eyes as he recalled April 4, 1968 and the days that followed. I could see that even after all these years, Nelson still hadn't recovered from the loss of his friend, a man he greatly admired.

Being around Martin, I learned a lot about courage, leadership, and what it meant to be a man. I've also learned over my eighty-four years on earth that sometimes you face adversity in life, and not because you messed up. Sometimes you're doing something right, and that bothers people. It bothered the Klan, the white supremacists, and many of the others who would rather see black people dead than treat us as equals. Across the country, many people were nervous about King. They understood that his ability to mobilize people was a very powerful asset, and that worried them. They realized that he was a very formidable leader and orator and someone who people felt comfortable following. After the bus boycotts ended in Montgomery, in 1956, all of us knew that he was more than just a person who could speak well in front of the pulpit; he was a capable leader.

I've read many times that his life was threatened constantly, and that there were even times when alleged assassins were waiting for him at events where by chance the event was cancelled, or for some reason he didn't make it there. I don't know if you call that luck or just that God was watching over him.

I would say that it was probably a little bit of both. Looking back, I think that it was almost unavoidable that he would get killed because of the position he was in as a leader. A target was always on his back,

every day. And as the civil rights movement evolved, the door opened up
even wider and invited in even more threats to his life.

The whole thing with Vietnam was a problem. Reverend King
started speaking out about the Vietnam War and that made even more
people despise him. For instance, in 1967, Reverend King returned
to Montgomery for an event and he stopped by the barbershop to get
a haircut. Even though he had moved to Atlanta a few years earlier,
anytime he was in Montgomery, he stopped by to say hello to me and my
brothers. One day, he had a bad run in with Coach Arthur Simmons,
who was the football coach at Alabama State College. This happened a
bit after Reverend King had preached a sermon at Riverside Church in
New York, criticizing the Vietnam War and President Johnson, and he'd
received a lot of negative press. Coach Simmons had a lot of admiration
for Lyndon Johnson and disagreed with the reverend about that issue.
So, Coach asked him, "Why did you go against Lyndon Johnson and his
foreign policy in your speech in New York? Lyndon Johnson is the best
thing that could have ever happened to black people. We got a civil rights
bill signed in 1964 and we got a voting rights bill in 1965. All of this
was done by Lyndon Johnson. What's wrong with you?"

Reverend King didn't appreciate the way that Coach Simmons was
talking to him, but he stayed calm and relaxed. He replied by saying,
"You know, Coach, my concern is not so much about American foreign
policy, my concern is that the president is a liar."

That's when Coach Simmons said, "Well, I don't know if you've realized
it yet, but two of America's biggest government contractors are General
Dynamics and Martin Marietta, and their biggest client is the US
Military. A lot of black people have jobs now because of this, so why are
you against Johnson?"

By now, Reverend King was getting angry, and so were some of the brothers in the barbershop. They were upset about the way Coach Simmons was speaking to a man they respected and had a lot of admiration for. When Reverend King turned around to walk out of the barbershop, Coach Simmons aggressively pointed his finger in his direction and said, "You're going to get yourself killed." That was in 1967, and sure enough . . .

The very last time that Martin came to the barbershop for a haircut was in late December of 1967. He had been invited back to Montgomery for the ninetieth anniversary celebration of Dexter Avenue Baptist Church, where he was once the pastor. All the former pastors were invited back for the celebration. When he stopped by the barbershop, he seemed like he was in good spirits. We didn't see any of those white boys parked outside either, so my brother asked him, "Where is your security?" We still didn't know yet that he didn't have security. We still didn't know that those white boys who used to be sitting in front of the barbershop sometimes when he arrived, were FBI agents.

So, Reverend King said, "The man upstairs is with me now." And those were the last words we heard him say in person: "The man upstairs is with me now." That was in December of 1967, and that's the last time I saw him alive. A few months later he went to Memphis, and you know the rest of the story.

———

In late summer of 2017, Nelson returned to Baltimore. He had been invited to an event to speak about the civil rights movement and his relationship with Martin Luther King Jr. It was an event like the one where he and I first met, several months earlier, and it felt nice to have him back in my hometown. I hadn't seen him since the last time I was in Montgomery, and I was looking forward to catching up. Throughout the time we spent together, Nelson was always an easy guy to have a conversation with, and I appreciated that. He was never judgmental and never made me feel like an idiot because I didn't know much about a time that I should have known well.

When I met up with Nelson, he told me that before arriving in Baltimore, he had been in New Haven, Connecticut, at Yale University. He was a guest speaker at an event held to honor his good friend Judge Myron H. Thompson for his outstanding public service. Judge Thompson was a graduate of the Yale Law School and he was being inducted into the Yale Honor Society. He now has the lengthy, but highly prestigious title of, "Senior United States District Judge for the US District Court for the Middle District of Alabama," a position he was appointed to in 1980 by President Jimmy Carter. Before becoming a federal judge, he was an assistant attorney general for Alabama. Nelson has several friends from Alabama who are well accomplished.

Nelson spoke with me about his time at Yale, and then the conversation branched out into how he wants more young people to understand the civil rights movement. He said this will help the next generation build on legislative and policy successes that make life better for African Americans. Nelson is like a walking handbook that comes with instructions on what to do and what not to do. He is also the ultimate motivator, and his presence alone makes you want to sit up straight and pull yourself together. He motivates me to want to do better for myself and for the world. His presence lit a fire in me, the way my grandfather's did before he passed away.

It was surreal seeing Nelson standing in front of a packed room, talking about the years he spent in the barbershop in Montgomery, at 407 S. Jackson Street, with many of the figures who were once part of a movement that changed America. I heard the same words that had piqued my interest months earlier and sent me on a journey into the past.

"I first met Reverend King in 1954, in Montgomery, Alabama ..." Nelson said to the fascinated audience at the Motor House Theatre in Baltimore—and with that, he once again began sharing knowledge that could change people's lives.

AFTERWORD: RACE IN AMERICA

I've never been called "nigger" to my face by a white man, so I can only imagine how I'd react in that situation. The face of racism in America today is different than that of yesterday's torch-carrying segregationists. It can be difficult to see until it rears its ugly head, like when a noose was found inside the National Museum of African American History and Culture in Washington, DC, or when the "n-word" was painted on the fence of NBA superstar LeBron James's multimillion-dollar home in Los Angeles. There was also the time Bill Maher was comfortable enough to use the "n-word" on primetime television and was not punished by HBO. There was also the time when award-winning journalist April Ryan was disrespected by the president of the United States when he asked her if she has "friends" in the Congressional Black Caucus and could "set up" a meeting with them, as if all black people are part of some secret society and personally acquainted with one another.

There is also often modern racism in the debate over the Confederate flag and monuments, cloaked in the argument of "historical respect." And there is violent racism, as in the case of a white man from Baltimore who travelled to New York for the express purpose of finding and killing black men. But the overt kinds are far less common than the covert, and overall, and today's racism is surreptitious, operating just outside the realm of our perception.

In some ways, the adaptation of American racism is encouraging. There is plenty of historical evidence of ideologies falling out of favor, moving to the outskirts of society, and then dying there like a wounded animal. But this has also made racism harder for us to track down, identify, and annihilate. To do so, we need to get to the source of racism in America, which for the most part is in the belly of white America.

Almost daily there's evidence of racism across the country, but it seems to me that as far as many white people are concerned, racism in America is over. They believe that the the angry, violent, and wide-ranging racism is something of the past; something that their grandparents' generation did that they have nothing to do with today.

Average white people don't consider themselves racists, and for the most part, they aren't—at least not stereotypical racists. Most would never call a black person a nigger. They're comforted in their moral evolution by the fact that they have black friends, or that they listen to black music, or that they have no problem driving through a predominantly black neighborhood. But despite what they think of themselves, the evidence shows that they are still less likely to hire a black person if the option is presented. The idea of institutionalized racism is an unpleasant historical footnote that they would prefer not to talk about, and that's part of the problem.

One of the biggest obstacles to having a serious conversation about race in America today is that it's often a struggle to talk about it with white people, or at least this has been my experience. I hear people say things like, "How can this still be a problem today? I'm not a racist, and no one that I know is a racist." Some people can feel personally attacked just by having a conversation about it. This mindset has created a cognitive dissonance among many white people, which has led to a large gap in the way that they perceive race in America compared to their black neighbors.

In 2016, the Pew Research Center conducted an extensive survey[80] on views of race and inequality in America held by different races. The results provide evidence of the disparity of perceptions. According to the survey: 88 percent of blacks said that America needs to continue making changes for blacks to have equal rights, while only 53 percent of whites said the same.

Eighty-four percent of blacks said they were treated less fairly than whites by the police, compared to 50 percent of whites who agreed. 46 percent of whites said that race relations in America are good, and 45 percent said they are bad. Among black people, 61 percent said that race relations were bad, and just 34 percent said that they were good. Interestingly, 41 percent of whites in the United States, compared to 22 percent of blacks, said there is too much attention paid to racial issues today.

The survey was confirmation that we have a long way to go regarding race relations in this country. According to the survey, 58 percent of African Americans believe that we're worse off financially than whites, while 37 percent of whites believe we're equally well off. And lastly, 70 percent of blacks say that racial discrimination is preventing us from getting ahead, but only 36 percent of whites agree.

That last statistic was the most revealing to me, and is damning evidence to support the idea that many white people continue to believe that black people's problems are *their own fault*. "This is America, after all, where anyone can be successful if they just commit themselves and work hard." What these people fail to understand is that the American dream is harder to achieve for a black person, not because of a lack

80   Pew Research Center's Social and Demographic Trends Project, "On Views of Race and Inequality, Blacks and Whites Are Worlds Apart," Pew Research Center, June 27, 2016.

of drive or ability, but because racism continues to exert influence on a system that creates real barriers to success. White Americans have a tough time understanding this because they don't feel it. It doesn't happen to them. If they can't see it, and they believe that they themselves aren't contributing to it, how can it still exist? When you believe that something doesn't exist, it's a lot easier to ignore it and rationalize it away, even when the results are easily visible.

There is a distinction between being bigoted—being someone who actively and consciously believes that people of a different race are inherently inferior—and being unconsciously racist, holding views and biases against people of color without awareness of doing so, and accepting without question a society and economy that quietly perpetuates inferior outcomes for people of color. But to accomplish what many people already believe—that racism in America has been solved—white people need to acknowledge that racism is still hurting minorities and that ultimately it won't be solved until they themselves begin to address it. Otherwise, it will continue to live just outside of our peripheral vision, and grow in strength and influence.

Being of African American descent and living in a country where we haven't always been treated fairly and haven't always felt as if we were getting our fair slice of this American pie has made many of us resentful. We've been under siege for some time now, and we have a long history of pain. From the American slave trade and Jim Crow laws to economic disparities, discriminatory housing, broken education systems, classism and more, it has always been a disproportionate struggle just for us to survive in America. We're still waiting for the equality, diversity, and inclusion that were promised by the United States Constitution. And despite the advances that have been made, those of us who came after the civil rights generation can't hope to make further progress if we allow ourselves to forget this fact. African

Americans have been sitting in the colored waiting room for many years, segregated from the American Dream, and we're still waiting for our turn.

There's no easy answer for what to do about racism, but the next step must be honesty. People of all colors must recognize modern racism, verbally admit its existence, and actively take steps to address it. We also need better education. No child, of any color, should grow up without a proper understanding of black history. Martin Luther King Jr. and many others made tremendous progress for African American rights, and I'm certain that if we look to the lessons they imparted, they will give us clues for how to navigate the future.

TIMELINE

For those readers whose knowledge of African American history is rusty at best, like mine before I met Nelson Malden, what follows is a timeline of some significant events. The timeline goes from slavery to modern times to give context to the state of black America today, and notes many of the events discussed in this book. In no way is this timeline complete, but I believe it aids with understanding where we're at and how we got here. I've closed with the death of Freddie Gray in my hometown of Baltimore, although the timeline could have kept going.

Many of the key events in African American history were turning points in our society at large, and others will forever be a stain on the pages of our history books, both those in print today and the ones still to be written: the ones that will include the events that unfold in our lifetime.

March 6, 1857

The US Supreme Court rules in *Dred Scott v. Sandford*, commonly known as "the Dred Scott decision," that *all* black people in America, slave or free, are "a subordinate and inferior class of beings," denying them citizenship and constitutional rights.

April 12, 1861

The Civil War begins with the Confederate attack on the Union-held Fort Sumter, in Charleston Harbor, South Carolina.

January 1, 1863

President Abraham Lincoln issues the Emancipation Proclamation, freeing slaves in the states that make up the Confederacy.

April 9, 1865

Though fighting will continue into the summer, the Civil War begins to reach its conclusion with the surrender of Confederate general Robert E. Lee to Union general Ulysses S. Grant in Appomattox, Virginia.

December 6, 1865

The Thirteenth Amendment to the United States Constitution is ratified, abolishing slavery. However, Southern states manage to revive slavery-era codes that prevent blacks from living, working, and participating in society on equal terms with whites by creating unattainable requirements.

July 9, 1868

The Fourteenth Amendment to the US Constitution is ratified, guaranteeing due process and equal protection under the law to all American citizens, including African Americans.

February 3, 1870

The Fifteenth Amendment to the US Constitution is ratified, stating that no US citizen shall be denied the right to vote "on account of race, color, or previous condition of servitude." States begin to institute other obstacles to turn away black voters, such as poll taxes and literacy tests.

March 1, 1875

Congress passes its third civil rights act since the Civil War, prohibiting racial discrimination and guaranteeing equal access to public accommodations, regardless of a person's race, in response to many white business owners and merchants who refused to make their facilities and establishments available to black people as well as whites. White supremacist groups begin concentrated campaigns against blacks and against whites who choose to obey the new laws.

May 18, 1896

The US Supreme Court's decision in *Plessy v. Ferguson* upholds a Louisiana statute that requires railroads to establish racially segregated but "equal" passenger cars. The court decides that racial segregation laws for public facilities are constitutional as long as the segregated facilities are equal in quality. This "separate but equal" doctrine legitimized Jim Crow laws and practices throughout the South for almost the next sixty years, until 1954.

February 12, 1909

The National Association for the Advancement of Colored People (NAACP) is founded in New York City by a multiracial group of activists including W. E. B. DuBois, Henry Moskowitz, Mary White Ovington, Oswald Garrison Villard, William English Walling, and Ida B. Wells.

May 17, 1954

The US Supreme Court's unanimous ruling in *Brown v. Board of Education of Topeka, Kansas* declares that segregated public education facilities are inherently unequal and therefore unconstitutional, overturning the precedent set by *Plessy v. Ferguson* and paving the way for desegregation. The case is a major victory for NAACP attorney Thurgood Marshall.

August 28, 1955

While visiting family in Mississippi, fourteen-year-old Chicago native Emmett Till is kidnapped and murdered for allegedly harassing a white woman, Carolyn Bryant. Bryant's husband, Roy, and his half-brother, J. W. Milam, are tried for the murder and acquitted by an all-white jury; they later boast in media interviews about committing the murder. Sixty years later, Bryant admits to author Timothy B. Tyson that her testimony in the trial was false, saying "Nothing that boy did could ever justify what happened to him."

December 1, 1955

Rosa Parks is arrested for refusing to give up her seat on a public bus in Montgomery, Alabama, to a white passenger. In response to her arrest, the black community in Montgomery launches a bus boycott led in part by Martin Luther King Jr., the newly elected president of the Montgomery Improvement Association and the pastor of the Dexter Avenue Baptist Church. The boycott lasts over a year, until a Supreme Court ruling on December 21, 1956 finds that segregation on public transportation is a violation of the Fourteenth Amendment.

February 14, 1957

The Southern Christian Leadership Conference, led by Martin Luther King Jr., Charles K. Steele, and Fred L. Shuttlesworth, is established, with King as its president. Its principles of nonviolence and protest through civil disobedience position it as a major force in organizing the civil rights movement.

September 2, 1957

Nine black students, now known as the "Little Rock Nine," are prevented from entering and integrating the formerly all-white Central High School in Little Rock, Arkansas, on the order of the state's governor, Orval Faubus. President Dwight Eisenhower intervenes. Three weeks later, Little Rock policemen surround Central High and escort the nine black students inside through a side door to avoid a mob of more than one thousand segregation supporters gathered in front of the school.

February 1, 1960

Four black university students from North Carolina Agricultural and Technical State University begin a sit-in at a segregated Woolworth's lunch counter in Greensboro, North Carolina. They are denied service, but they return day after day alongside a growing number of African Americans—dozens, and then hundreds—who refuse to leave the lunch counter, paralyzing it and other local businesses. The event triggers similar protests throughout the South at public facilities including libraries, parks, and swimming pools. Six months later, the Greensboro Four are served lunch at the Woolworth's counter where the protest began.

April 1960

The Student Nonviolent Coordinating Committee is founded at Shaw University in Raleigh, North Carolina, and soon becomes a prominent organizing force of young blacks, including future congressman John Lewis. In the late 1960s, under the leadership of Stokely Carmichael and H. Rap Brown, the organization develops a more radical bent, changing its name to the Student National Coordinating Committee.

March 6, 1961

President John F. Kennedy signs Executive Order 10925, prohibiting federal government agencies from discrimination based on race, religion, or national origin, whether in the hiring process or during an employee's tenure, and establishing the President's Committee on Equal Employment Opportunity to scrutinize the federal government's employment practices.

June 12, 1963

At thirty-seven years old, NAACP field secretary Medgar Evers is murdered outside his home in Jackson, Mississippi. In 1964, Byron De La Beckwith is twice tried for the crime, with both trials resulting in hung juries. Thirty years later, in 1994, De La Beckwith is tried again based on a new investigation, and is convicted of murdering Evers.

August 28, 1963

More than 250,000 people attend the March on Washington on the National Mall in Washington, DC. From the steps of the Lincoln Memorial, Martin Luther King Jr. delivers his now world-famous "I Have a Dream" speech.

September 15, 1963

Denise McNair, Cynthia Wesley, Carole Robertson, and Addie Mae Collins—whose ages range between eleven and fourteen—are killed when a bomb explodes at the 16th Street Baptist Church, in Birmingham, Alabama, a popular location for civil rights meetings. Riots erupt, resulting in the deaths of two more black youths.

January 23, 1964

The Twenty-Fourth Amendment to the US Constitution abolishes the poll tax.

Summer 1964

A coalition of four civil rights groups, organizes the Freedom Summer project with the goal of registering black voters in Mississippi. The Congress of Racial Equality begins sending student volunteers on bus trips to test new laws prohibiting segregation in interstate travel facilities. The "Freedom Riders," as they are called, are met with protest and violence. By the end of the summer, more than one thousand volunteers, both black and white, have participated in the program. The Congress of Racial Equality also sends delegates to the 1964 Democratic National Convention under the banner of the Mississippi Freedom Democratic Party to protest the official all-white delegation from the state.

July 2, 1964

President Lyndon B. Johnson signs the sweeping Civil Rights Act of 1964, which prohibits discrimination of any kind based on race, color, religion, or national origin in public facilities, government, and employment and allows the federal government to enforce deseg-regation. The signing of the law finally begins to loosen the grip of Jim Crow laws in the South and the government's power to enforce the act grows over time, laying the groundwork for later programs, such as affirmative action, which aimed to repair some of the social and economic damage to the lives of blacks caused by longstanding segregation and discrimination.

August 4, 1964

The bodies of three young civil rights workers, James Chaney, Andrew Goodman, and Mickey Schwerner—are found near Philadelphia,

Mississippi. The men had disappeared on June 21, having been arrested on an alleged traffic violation, and then released after dark, at which point they were pursued and murdered by two carloads of members of the Ku Klux Klan. The state of Mississippi declines to issue any indictments, but the FBI ultimately charges eighteen men with conspiracy to violate the civil rights of the victims. Five are convicted, eight are acquitted, and the trial of three more ends in a deadlock from the all-white jury. More than forty years later, on June 21, 2005, one man, Edgar Ray Killen, is convicted on three counts of manslaughter and sentenced to sixty years in prison.

February 21, 1965

Born Malcolm Little in Omaha, Nebraska, on May 19, 1925, Malcolm X went on to become a world-renowned black nationalist leader, civil rights activist, and sometime spokesman for the Nation of Islam who famously advocated for black freedom "by any means necessary." On February 21, 1965, at thirty-nine years old, Malcolm X is assassinated at the Audubon Ballroom in Harlem while delivering a speech. In March 1966, three members of the Nation of Islam, Talmadge Hayer, Norman 3X Butler, and Thomas 15X Johnson, are convicted of his murder.

March 7, 1965

In an event that will come to be known as "Bloody Sunday," blacks determined to march in support of voting rights from Selma, Alabama, to Montgomery, are stopped by a police blockade at the Edmund Pettus Bridge in Selma. In the presence of the news media, state troopers, the Dallas County Sheriff's Department, and numerous white citizens deputized by Sheriff Jim Clark attack the peaceful demonstrators with billy clubs, teargas, and bullwhips. Each of the three television networks interrupts its telecasts to broadcast footage of the inhumane violence, catalyzing public opinion among both black and white Americans in support of the marchers.

March 9, 1965

Two days after Bloody Sunday, demonstrations in support of the marchers are held in eighty cities across America. Thousands of supporters arrive in Selma to undertake a second march, but this time, Martin Luther King Jr. leads the marchers to the Edmund Pettus Bridge, where they kneel, pray, and then return to the Brown Chapel A.M.E Church in Selma. The decision to turn around follows a federal court judge's restraining order on the march and, in its aftermath, King's negotiations with a representative of President Lyndon B. Johnson, who was concerned about another outbreak of violence. The event becomes known as "Turnaround Tuesday." That night, a white Northern Unitarian Universalist minister, James Reeb, who was in Selma to march, is attacked by white vigilantes. He dies of his wounds two days later.

March 21–25, 1965

Under the protection of the National Guard, federalized by President Lyndon B. Johnson over the objections of Alabama Governor George Wallace, voting rights advocates complete their intended march from Selma to Montgomery, where more than twenty-five thousand people gather before the state capitol on March 25.

August 10, 1965

Literacy tests, poll taxes, and similar requirements that restrict blacks from voting are declared broadly illegal when Congress passes the Voting Rights Act, guaranteeing every American twenty-one years old and over the right to vote, thus making it easier for Southern blacks to register. The passage of the act is seen as a direct consequence of the events in Alabama five months earlier.

September 24, 1965

President Lyndon B. Johnson signs Executive Order 11246, requiring government contractors to "take affirmative action" toward prospective minority employees in all aspects of hiring and employment. (Two years later, Executive Order 11375, issued by Johnson on October 13, 1967, extends the language of this order to include women.)

June 12, 1967

The Supreme Court's decision in *Loving v. Virginia* declares bans on interracial marriage unconstitutional, forcing sixteen states with such bans still in place to strike them from their lawbooks.

August 30, 1967

The appointment by President Lyndon B. Johnson of Thurgood Marshall, who successfully argued *Brown v. Board of Education* on behalf of the NAACP, as the first African American justice of the United States, is confirmed by the Senate.

April 4, 1968

At age thirty-nine, Rev. Dr. Martin Luther King Jr. is assassinated at the Lorraine Motel in Memphis, Tennessee. As African Americans grieve, riots and fires ensue in cities across America. To avoid possible execution if convicted by jury trial, prior convict and committed racist James Earl Ray pleads guilty to the murder.

April 11, 1968

The Civil Rights Act of 1968 is signed into law by President Lyndon B. Johnson. It prohibits discrimination in the rental, sale, and financing of housing in America, formally rendering racially restrictive covenants in property deeds illegal, though social and financial obstacles for African Americans in obtaining fair housing continue.

April 20, 1971

The Supreme Court's decision in *Swann v. Charlotte-Mecklenburg Board of Education* upholds busing—sending public-school students from predominantly black neighborhoods to schools in predominantly white neighborhoods—as a legitimate means of achieving school integration. Though unpopular among whites (and sometimes met with violence), court-ordered busing plans continue through the 1990s in cities such as Charlotte, Boston, and Denver.

June 28, 1978

In *Regents of the University of California v. Bakke*, the Supreme Court upholds the right of universities to consider race as a factor in admissions so long as no racial quotas are established, confirming the constitutionality of affirmative-action policies.

March 22, 1988

Congress passes the Civil Rights Restoration Act, overriding President Ronald Reagan's veto, to expand the reach of nondiscrimination laws within private institutions that receive federal funds.

September 21, 1989

General Colin Powell becomes the first African American chairman of the Joint Chiefs of Staff, the highest post in the United States Military.

June 23, 1992

Declaring that the consideration of race in admissions furthers "a compelling interest in obtaining the educational benefits that flow from a diverse student body," the Supreme Court upholds the affirmative-action policy of the University of Michigan Law School, in the Court's most important decision regarding race and educational policy since *Regents of the University of California v. Bakke*, in 1978.

March 3, 1991

Rodney King, an African American motorist, is stopped by Los Angeles police officers after an eight-mile pursuit, and then severely beaten by four officers while others officers watch. George Holliday, an area resident, captures the beating on a handheld video recorder and sends it to a local news station. Parts of the video are broadcast around the world.

April 29, 1992

A jury trial acquits the four officers charged with excessive force in the arrest and beating of Rodney King. A series of riots, called the "Los Angeles Riots," ensue, in which thousands of people loot stores, burn property, and engage in civil unrest for six straight days. An estimated one billion dollars in damages to the city are reported. Nearly twelve thousand people are arrested during the riots, more than two thousand are injured, and more than fifty are killed.[81]

October 16, 1995

The Million Man March, organized by Louis Farrakhan, the controversial leader of the Nation of Islam, is held in Washington, DC, to promote African American unity. Estimates on the number of attendees, mostly African American men, are between 400,000 and 1.1 million.[82] Speakers include Jesse Jackson, Rosa Parks, and Martin Luther King III. Atonement, responsibility, and reconciliation are emphasized.

October 25, 1997

The Million Woman March, founded by grassroots activist Phile Chionesu, takes place in Philadelphia, to promote solidarity and family unity in African American communities. Police estimate an attendance of between 300,000 and 1 million people.[83] Speakers include Winnie Madikizela-Mandela, the ex-wife of Nelson Mandela; Congresswoman Maxine Waters; Jada Pinkett Smith; and Attallah and Ilyasah Shabazz, the daughters of Malcolm X.

---

81   CNN Library, CNN.com, updated April 23, 2017.

82   Editors of *Encyclopædia Britannica*, "Million Man March," *Encyclopedia Brittanica*, accessed January 28, 2018.

83   CNN Editors, "Million Woman March Fills Philadelphia Streets," CNN.com, October 27, 1997.

Janurary 26, 2005

Condoleezza Rice is appointed Secretary of State. She is the first female African American to hold the position.

November 4, 2008

Barack Obama becomes the first African American president of the United States. Young black voters go to the polls in greater proportion than young voters in other ethnic groups, and black women turnout is at a higher rate than any other racial, ethnic, and gender group. The historic gap between black and white voter participation is nearly closed.[84]

February 26, 2012

Seventeen-year-old Trayvon Martin is shot and killed by George Zimmerman in Sanford, Florida, sparking a national debate on "stand your ground laws" and the shooting of unarmed black men. Zimmerman is later charged with second-degree murder and acquitted in a jury trial. President Barack Obama calls Martin's death a "tragedy" and says, "If I had a son, he would look like Trayvon."

November 6, 2012

Barack Obama is reelected president of the United States. For the first time, black voter turnout rate exceeds white voter turnout rate. A record high of 66.6% of black Americans go to the polls.[85]

---

84 Sam Roberts, "2008 Surge in Black Voters Nearly Erased Racial Gap" *New York Times*, July 20, 2009.

85 Krogstad and Lopez, "Black Voter Turnout Fell in 2016, Even as a Record Number of Americans Cast Ballots."

July 13, 2013

Alicia Garza, Opal Tometi, and Patrisse Cullors create the hashtag Black Lives Matter following the acquittal of George Zimmerman in the death of Trayvon Martin. Black Lives Matter becomes a member-led organization and activist movement focused on building strength in black communities and responding to violence inflicted on their members. It becomes globally recognized for its street demonstrations in protests following the death of young black men.

June 17, 2015

A twenty-one-year-old gunman, Dylann Roof, kills nine African American worshippers inside a historic black church in Charleston, South Carolina. Roof is later convicted of the murders and thirty-three federal hate crimes. On January 19, 2017, he is sentenced to death. Roof told investigators that he had intended to start a race war.[86]

August 9–10, 2014

Eighteen-year-old Michael Brown is shot and killed by police in Ferguson, Missouri. Police and a friend of Brown's, who was with him at the time of the murder, disagree on the circumstances that led up to the shooting, but agree that Brown was unarmed. The next day, riots begin in response to the shooting. Businesses are looted, and police respond dressed in armor and riot gear. President Barack Obama calls Brown's death, "heartbreaking," but asks the residents of Ferguson to be patient as the investigation unfolds. The unrest in Ferguson lasts ten days.

---

86   Ray Sanchez and Ed Payne, "Charleston Church Shooting: Who is Dylann Roof?" CNN, December 16, 2016.

July 17, 2014

Forty-three-year-old Eric Garner dies in Staten Island, New York, after being placed in a chokehold by a police officer. Ramsey Orta, a friend of Garner's, records the incident on his cell phone and the video later goes viral. Five months later, a grand jury declines to indict the officer, sparking protests in New York, with tens of thousands of protesters pouring into the streets, and cities across the country.

April 4, 2015

Fifty-year-old Walter Scott is shot multiple times by officer Michael Slager in Charleston, South Carolina, following a traffic stop for a nonfunctioning brake light. Initially, Slager stated that Scott attempted to take away his service weapon, but cell phone footage recorded by a witness proved that false. Slager would later be sentenced to twenty years in prison following a plea agreement.

April 19, 2015

Twenty-five-year-old Freddie Gray dies from a spinal cord injury while in the custody of the Baltimore City Police Department, sparking a violent uprising in the city. Maryland Governor Larry Hogan declares a State of Emergency and activates the Maryland National Guard and Baltimore Mayor Stephanie Rawlings-Blake imposes a citywide curfew. Charges against the officers are later dropped or they are found not guilty. Later, the US Justice Department begins an investigation into the Baltimore Police Department and finds that it disproportionately harms African Americans. An agreement outlines a plan for change that includes more community outreach.[87]

87   Department of Justice, Office of Public Affairs, "Justice Department Announces Findings of Investigation Into Baltimore Police Department," August 10, 2016.

ACKNOWLEDGMENTS

In my view, there are two things that most define you as a person: your patience when you have nothing and your attitude when you have everything. Every morning when I wake up I clearly understand that I've travelled a long way in my life, but I also know that I'm still a work in progress. Personal growth only manifests itself fully when you have people around you who challenge you, as well as people who show you the path. Here are some of the individuals who have shown me the path over the years and who have helped me stay focused. These are also the folks who have helped me refocus and reframe, to avoid getting distracted by all the noise in the world: my daughter and *Star Wars* movie partner, Brooke Shird; my fellow New York Knicks fan, Alex Gordon; my homegirl from another world, Tia Gasgue; my Muslim brother, Moses Hammett; my friend and brother, Wes Moore; my occasional lunch date, Joy Thomas Moore; my good friend and runway fashion stylist from West Baltimore, Toni James; the brain Nicole Kirby; my homegirl, Khayla Dorsey, whom I always text message for a good laugh when I'm bored in a long meeting; my shoulder to lean on, Terrie M. Williams; my social media aficionado, Cynthia Todd; and rest in peace to my friend and writing mentor, Mr. Gregory Kane. Thank you to my Philadelphia brother and mentor, Abdul Hakim Ali; my sister, Wanda

Shird; my nephew Zegory Crawley; my nephew Brandon Crawley; my father, Charles Shird; my mother, Brenda Mills; my brother, Karl Shird; my sister, Karen Shird; my third nephew Ryan Shird; my barber, Keon Evans; the quiet storm, Nina Keyes; my lunch buddy, Dr. Steve Sobelman; my lunch buddy's wife, Sloan Brown; the godfather, Glen Middleton; my guy, Charles Reynolds; my friend, David Warnock; my friend and barber, Derick "Razorblade" Ausby; Marisol "Insurance Lady" Johnson; Bilal Ali; my California desert walking buddy, Malik; my publishers, Julia Abramoff and Alex Merrill; editor Molly Pisani; publicist Justin Loeber; my friend in Alabama, Mr. Nelson Malden; my good friend Shelonda Stokes; and my incredible daughter, Kiara Dunn.

Nelson at eighteen, in his high school graduation gown.

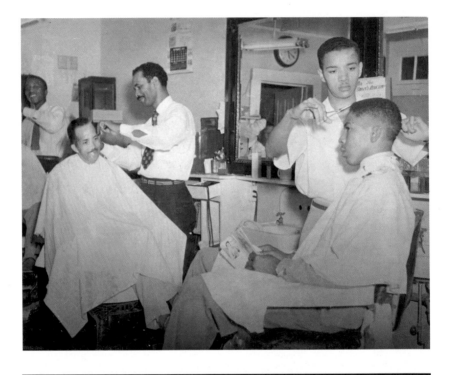

Nelson (right) at nineteen, inside the College Hill Barbershop. His brothers, Spurgeon (center) and Stephen (left), are behind him.

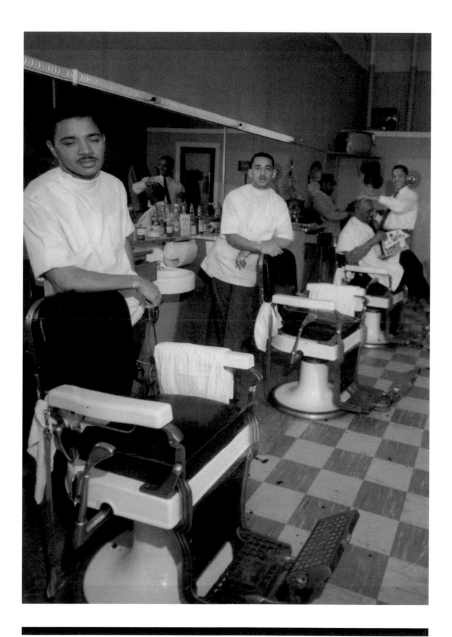

Nelson, Stephen, and Spurgeon by their chairs in the Malden Brothers Barbershop.

Elect

NELSON MALDEN

DEMOCRATIC EXECUTIVE
COMMITTEEMAN

Qualified
for the
Position

- BA Degree Political Science
  Alabama State College
- 20 Years Business Experience
  (with the Public)
- Honorably Discharged
  Veteran U. S. Navy
- Member Institute of General Semantics
- Faithful Member Dexter Avenue
  Baptist Church
- Enjoys Working with People

(Pd. Pol. Adv. by Nelson Malden)

VOTE MALDEN
(MARCH 20th, 1966)
and Keep the Faith

An advertisement for Nelson from when he ran for public office.

Rev. Dr. Martin Luther King Jr. speaking at the YMCA's Father-Son Banquet on December 5, 1955.

Marchers during the third Selma to Montgomery March that commenced on March 17, 1965. This march received federal protection.

Troopers watch the marchers during the third Selma to Montgomery March.

Marchers in the rain during the third Selma to Montgomery March. The fifty-four mile march took five days.

Nelson (right) in the funeral procession for Rev. Dr. Martin Luther King Jr. in Atlanta on April 9, 1968.

Rev. Dr. Martin Luther King Jr.'s casket in the Atlanta funeral procession.

Mourners in the funeral procession for Rev. Dr. Martin Luther King Jr.

The "Colored Waiting Room" sign in the Malden Brothers Barbershop. It was used in a train station in the days of segregation.

MUSTACHE _____ 10.0
BEARD CUT & SHAPED 5.00
EYEBROW ARCH 11.0(
SHAMPOO _____ 7.0(
RELAXER _____ 6.0(
HAIR DYE _____ 17.0(
17.0(

Kevin in Nelson's chair in the Malden Brothers Barbershop.

Kevin speaking with boys in Baltimore City.

Kevin leading a workshop at a Baltimore City high school.

Kevin and Nelson.